Praise for *Ruthless Consistency* and Michael Canic

Great leaders pursue strategic change with the commitment of a world-class athlete. Every CEO should read *Ruthless Consistency* to learn the difference between success and failure.
—**Sam Reese**, CEO, Vistage Worldwide, Inc.

Ruthless Consistency equips you with the tools to be the exception to the trend of failed strategic change initiatives. This is the ultimate guide to implementing real, positive, and lasting change in your organization.
—**Marshall Goldsmith**, Thinkers 50 #1 Executive Coach and only two-time #1 Leadership Thinker

It's all about commitment. If we didn't adopt ruthless consistency, we wouldn't have achieved 10 years of double-digit CAGR and built a team that is focused, mentally tough, and able to execute.
—**Kurt Lang**, President, Air Technologies

Ruthless Consistency isn't just a book; it's a road map for unlocking your organization's potential. Michael's approach awakened our leadership team, resulting in a more engaged, productive, and profitable organization—and we had a lot more fun doing it.
—**Michelle Gleeson**, EVP and COO, Gulfshore Insurance

Committing to Michael's approach was the single best investment of time and money I made as a CEO. I just wish I had done it 20 years earlier.
—**Riyaz Devji**, CEO, North American Tea & Coffee

Leaders must be disciplined and focused to succeed in today's economy. Ruthless consistency is the key, and Michael Canic provides the blueprint.

—**Todd Millar**, President and CEO, TEC Canada

Every CEO who wants to pivot their company needs to read this book. It's a proven playbook for leaders to connect their strategy to the holistic culture change needed to drive a sustained commitment to win.

—**Margo Georgiadis**, President and CEO, Ancestry.com

When I came into this role, we needed a strategy and a surefire way to execute. Ruthless consistency provided it. Now, seeing the results, we have the foundation and the confidence to really think big.

—**Matt Lewis**, President, Braidy Corporation

Ruthless Consistency offers a strategic guide for organizations to achieve their full potential. Michael emphasizes the importance of focus, teamwork, and unwavering commitment. These were key ingredients that helped me complete my Man in Motion World Tour.

—**Rick Hansen**, Founder, Rick Hansen Foundation

Everything we do now is built around consistency—the right focus, the right environment, and the right team. It's allowed us to scale, and we have the results to show for it. If you're serious about growing your business, then you need to read this book.

—**Tony Mazzella**, CEO, Mazzella Companies

Ruthless consistency is the relentless and disciplined pursuit of a clearly defined and shared purpose. The prerequisite is a serious leader with serious mental toughness; not for the faint of heart.

—**Freda Cheung**, EVP, Dufry North America

RUTHLESS
CONSISTENCY

RUTHLESS
CONSISTENCY

How Committed Leaders Execute Strategy, Implement Change, and Build Organizations That Win

MICHAEL CANIC, PHD

New York   Chicago   San Francisco   Athens   London
Madrid   Mexico City   Milan   New Delhi
Singapore   Sydney   Toronto

1 2 3 4 5 6 7 8 9   LCR   25 24 23 22 21 20

ISBN   978-1-260-45981-4
MHID   1-260-45981-0

e-ISBN   978-1-260-45982-1
e-MHID   1-260-45982-9

Library of Congress Cataloging-in-Publication Data

Names: Canic, Michael, author.
Title: Ruthless consistency : how committed leaders execute strategy,
    implement change, and build organizations that win / Michael Canic, PhD.
Description: New York City : McGraw Hill, 2020. | Includes bibliographical
    references and index.
Identifiers: LCCN 2020022594 (print) | LCCN 2020022595 (ebook) |
    ISBN 9781260459814 (hardback) | ISBN 9781260459821 (ebook)
Subjects: LCSH: Organizational change. | Strategic planning. | Personnel
    management. | Leadership.
Classification: LCC HD58.8 .C32166 2020 (print) | LCC HD58.8 (ebook) |
    DDC 658.4/092—dc23
LC record available at https://lccn.loc.gov/2020022594
LC ebook record available at https://lccn.loc.gov/2020022595

To Bernadine,
"who lights the meaning of his life"

CONTENTS

PREFACE

I WANT TO MAKE YOU UNCOMFORTABLE. I want to bring you face-to-face with what you haven't done but need to do for your organization to win. I want to provoke a smoldering discontent for the way things are and a fierce resolve to change them.

If you're a leader who has had enough of strategic plans that go off the rails, change initiatives that flounder, or chronic underperformance, then this book is for you. This book is also for you if you're a leader or aspiring leader who is ambitious and committed to fulfilling your ambitions.

I wrote *Ruthless Consistency* with middle-market companies in mind. My experience and expertise as a strategy + execution consultant is rooted almost entirely in this segment, a segment that is largely ignored in the business literature yet accounts for one-third of the private-sector economy. These aren't the big behemoths or sexy startups; yet many of these fly-under-the-radar companies are some of the best companies you've never heard of. And while *Ruthless Consistency* was written with an eye to the mid-market, many of the principles and practices apply to organizations of all sizes, including those outside of business, such as in education and the not-for-profit world.

Part I, "The Reality," sets the stage. It makes the case for three principles that you must understand and embrace to maximize your chances for success.

Part II, "The Right Focus," is where the applied journey begins. Simply put, without focus, your organization can't win. In this section, my intent is to have you reject strategic planning and commit to strategic management, a comprehensive and far more robust approach to developing and sustaining focus.

In Part III, "The Right Environment," I detail a model that shows how every organizational touchpoint must be consistent with winning. Practices and processes are provided to help manage those touchpoints.

In Part IV, "The Right Team," I outline successful approaches to the two processes fundamental to building the right team: recruitment and selection.

You might question why "The Right Environment" comes before "The Right Team." After all, once you're clear on what your organization must achieve, shouldn't you put the right team in place to achieve it? If you were starting from scratch, building a new team, then yes. But most organizations already have a team in place and leaders often believe they have the right team. The truth is, you won't fully know until you've created the right environment. Once you have, most team members will thrive, and engagement and performance will soar. However, it will also expose those who aren't willing or able to meet what's expected of them. In any event, don't think of these two parts of the book as strictly sequential. Creating the right environment and building the right team are both ongoing and iterative processes.

Part V, "The Right Commitment," shines the spotlight on you. Knowing what you need to do is one thing; having the will to do it is another. The chapters in this section identify the enemies of commitment, along with practical and proven ways to overcome them.

Expect *Ruthless Consistency* to challenge your thinking and your assumptions. Expect to have your level of commitment challenged. And expect to be equipped with models, methods, practices, and processes—all based on real-world experience—that will help you transform ambition into strategy, and strategy into reality.

Don't just read this book. *Reflect* on how it relates to your experience. And *preflect* on how you can and will apply what you've read and what you expect to happen as a result. Make notes, highlight, discuss with others, exchange stories . . . don't just read this book.

Why go down this path with me? Because for the past 20+ years I've worked with hundreds of CEOs and other executives making strategy happen. The principles and practices of *Ruthless Consistency* have been forged by hammering away at real-world challenges across a wide range of contexts.

Imagine that you and I are handcuffed together in the desert, dying of thirst. Off in the distance is an oasis. Each of us has to walk so that both of us can get there. If you stop walking, I won't be able to drag you there. If I stop walking, you won't be able to drag me there. I can't promise you that we'll make it to the oasis. But I can promise you that I won't be the one to stop.

Take your first step. Turn the page.

RUTHLESS
CONSISTENCY

INTRODUCTION
When All Is Said and Done,
a Lot More Gets Said Than Done*

IF YOU WANT TO PLAY the odds, bet on failure. That's what's likely to happen when you execute strategy or implement organizational change.

I've seen it play out countless times. Like when I managed the Consulting Division of The Atlanta Consulting Group. We would facilitate strategic planning retreats for mid-market companies. Working with the members of a client's Strategic Leadership Team, we would lead them through a structured process to develop their strategic plan. When we were done, they would be focused, aligned, and ready to conquer the world. Mission accomplished. Or so we thought.

The following year they would bring us back to help update their strategic plan. Naturally, we would ask what was accomplished the previous year. That's when the bodies would start to squirm and the eyes dart away.

Aesop.

"Well, we had hoped to accomplish more, but (insert list of excuses)."

The long and short of it: Not a lot got done.

Strategic planning? It was a charade. A waste of time, money, and effort. And our experience wasn't unique. Published failure rates for strategic planning range from 70 to 90 percent.[1]

FAILURE IS PERVASIVE, PAINFUL, AND PERSISTENT

It's not just strategic planning. The same is true of *any* strategic change initiative (SCI). Mergers and acquisitions? Up to 90 percent fail.[2] Lean Six Sigma? Between 60 and 90 percent fail.[3] Software and systems projects? Over 70 percent fail.[4]

And how costly is all this failure? For IT projects alone, the worldwide cost has been estimated at up to $3 trillion a year.[5] Yes, trillion with a "t."

Think of a failed SCI in your organization. Now guesstimate the *total cost of failure*—not just the up-front costs but also the downstream costs such as lost productivity, employee turnover, or lost customers. Now add the opportunity cost of failure. I'll bet the total cost of failure is far greater than you first thought.

This isn't a recent trend. A *Harvard Business Review* article noted that "most studies still show a 60–70 percent failure rate for organizational change projects—a statistic that has stayed constant from the 1970s to the present."[6]

Sure, you could quibble about the percentages or the definitions of failure, but the *conclusion* is undeniable. It doesn't matter whether it's strategic planning, an acquisition, IT implementation, or any of a thousand other SCIs. If you want to play the odds, bet on failure.

THE UNINTENDED, UNRECOGNIZED, AND UNFORGIVABLE CONSEQUENCES OF FAILURE

It gets worse. When SCIs repeatedly fail, you create a track record of failure. You create an *expectation* of failure. You create an *acceptance* of failure. And you create a *culture* of failure. Failure becomes the norm.

You might be thinking: "Hold on. It's not like our efforts have been a total failure. We've made progress. We've gotten some things done."

That's it? That's your reaction? And you're the leader?

The tragedy of repeated failures is how they poison organizational culture. It becomes easy for people—starting with you—to rationalize anything other than success. And it becomes all but impossible to get people to believe in and support the next SCI. The culture of failure becomes self-perpetuating.

Enough.

If you've decided that this travesty has to end, and you're intent on getting to the root of the issue, then take a look in the mirror.

It's you. It's what you as a leader *haven't done but need to do* to execute strategy, implement change, and build an organization that wins.

Here's the good news: This book can help you win. But *you* have to supply the commitment. It won't be easy and it won't happen overnight. Anyone who tells you otherwise either is lying or hasn't lived it.

First, I need to lay some groundwork to help you understand *why* SCIs so often fail, and the three surprising principles you must embrace to succeed.

Ready to face reality?

PART I

THE REALITY

Learn to see things as they really are,
not as we imagine they are.

—Vernon Howard

Most strategic change initiatives (SCIs) fail, but why? It's because leaders don't have a complete picture of reality: what it takes to execute strategic change, their role in making it happen, and the level of commitment required.

If you're fed up with failure, then first you need to understand the reality of why things fail.

FIRST PRINCIPLE
What Matters More Than Anything You Do Is *Everything* You Do

It's the little details that are vital. Little things make big things happen.

—John Wooden

"CREATE A CULTURE of continuous quality improvement."

That was the mandate that came down from corporate. It was early in my career with FedEx where I had taken on a role with responsibility for district-level service quality. I was just one of many young professionals at the company who wanted to make their mark in this newly created position.

FedEx already had a strong reputation for service quality. It had set the industry standard for reliability—delivering overnight packages "absolutely, positively" on-time—but the competition was closing the gap. Driven to stay one step ahead, the company decided to create a culture of continuous quality improvement, a culture that would continually find ways to enhance service, compress cycle times, and reduce costs. Better. Faster. Cheaper.

Many of my counterparts wanted to get a fast start. Almost immediately they started pushing people through quality training and forming quality teams. The race to implement quality was obvious when they reported their progress each month on a global conference call. Everyone wanted to impress.

I took a different approach. I knew that many organizations had gone down the same path, and while some had succeeded, most had failed. In fact, leading publications were touting headlines that suggested quality—known more commonly then as Total Quality Management, or TQM—was on its last legs: "TQM: More Than a Dying Fad?" (*Fortune*), "Is Quality Dead?" (*Training* magazine), "Totaled Quality Management" (*Washington Post*), "The Dark Side of Quality" (*Quality Digest*). Failure, apparently, was the norm. I wanted to know why. So instead of racing off to implement quality, I dove into the articles and case studies to understand what led to success and what led to failure.

Naturally, I had some preconceptions. All of them were wrong.

THE ANATOMY OF SUCCESS AND FAILURE

My first thought was that training was the key. Maybe the successful companies provided employees with more training than the unsuccessful ones. Maybe they delivered "just-in-time" training. Maybe they started by training top-level managers and then cascaded training down through the organization. All reasonable ideas . . . but none of them was the answer. Many companies provided quality training in a variety of ways, yet still failed.

Could it be resources? Maybe the successful companies simply allocated more resources to their quality efforts. But that wasn't it either. Surprisingly, the companies that applied the most resources often experienced the greatest failures.

What about communications? Maybe the secret was to communicate continually to employees the *what*, *why*, and *how* of continuous quality improvement. No, that wasn't it. I came across companies that implemented detailed communications plans . . . and still failed.

Incentives and rewards? Surely, aligning these with the desired behaviors and outcomes would lead to success. Nope. Measurement, tracking, and reporting? Same thing. And so it went with *every* management practice I examined. It all pointed to a conclusion I didn't like and didn't want to accept. That succeeding or failing with continuous quality improvement was simply a matter of chance.

I was at a dead end. Isn't there anything an organization can do that reliably leads to success?

And then it hit me. No, there isn't anything. *Any one thing.* It's everything. *Everything matters.*

Companies that successfully implemented continuous quality improvement made sure *everything* was aligned with success. Every decision. Every action. All the arrows were pointed in the right direction. Consistently.

The successful companies regularly communicated the purpose of continuous quality improvement, why it was important, and how it applied to each individual. They provided the necessary skills, resources, and authority. They developed metrics and goals. They tracked and reported progress. They aligned management compensation. They celebrated successes. And they had the courage to hold people accountable. Again, all the arrows were consistently pointed in the right direction. These companies understood that "tell 'em and train 'em" simply wasn't good enough. They knew that *any* critical factor misaligned could lead to failure.

And the companies that weren't successful? *Every* case of failure I came across could be traced to inconsistency. The unsuccessful companies formed quality improvement teams, but didn't give people the authority to make changes. They set goals, but didn't provide the resources to achieve them. They promoted quality, but as long as managers hit their financial targets, then quality didn't matter. Inconsistency.

It was absolutely clear. *The difference between success and failure was ruthless consistency.*

It turns out that's true not just for continuous quality improvement; it's true for *any* strategic change initiative (SCI). Successful implementation requires more than just a pinch of training, a dash of resources, and a dollop of communications. It requires a *systematic approach to aligning everything with the desired outcome.* Everything matters. The whole truly is greater than the sum of its parts.

Think of it this way. It takes only one misaligned wheel to make your car undrivable, one misaligned vertebra in your back to incapacitate you. *One misaligned element in any system can undermine everything.*

Ruthless consistency is the key to implementing strategic change.

A MODEL FOR RUTHLESS CONSISTENCY

Saying that everything needs to be consistently aligned is one thing, but doing it is another. To be ruthlessly consistent you have to *do* three things: Develop the *right focus.* Create the *right environment.* Build the *right team.* Continually. That's it. Every SCI always comes down to those three things.

Developing the right focus means identifying and articulating *why* your organization must change, *what* you intend to achieve,

Ruthless Consistency®

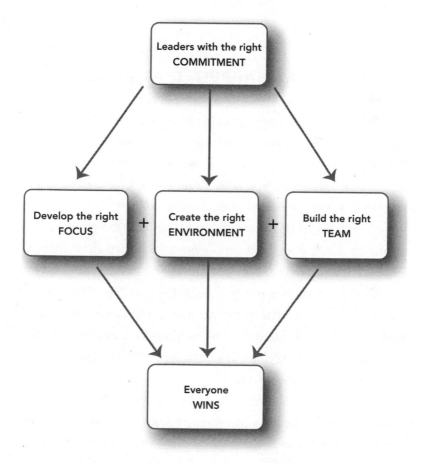

and *how* you intend to achieve it. Creating the right environment means aligning *every* organizational touchpoint, so that your team can and will execute on the right focus. Building the right team means securing the right *collection* of talent to make it happen.

Three things. But within those three things are a thousand opportunities to fail. Which is why I've devoted a full part of this book to each.

SO, WHAT HAPPENED AT FEDEX?

At FedEx, the compelling reason to change (the "why") was to stay one step ahead of our ever-improving competition. The intent (the "what") was to create a culture of continuous quality improvement to enhance service, compress cycle times, and reduce costs. The approach, at the corporate level (the macro "how"), was to put in place a structure of quality professionals, provide them with access to quality training and support materials, and then allow them to carry out the mandate as they saw fit. A good start but only a start.

I wanted to test the principles of ruthless consistency and create an environment that was aligned with our intentions, one in which people were focused, equipped, coached, and supported. I also wanted to form Quality Teams with people who had the right capabilities and traits to execute.

We succeeded. We documented numerous "Quality Success Stories" outlining how we had met the goals of enhanced service, compressed cycle times, and reduced costs. The result was that ours became the most successful and recognized district in the Americas for service quality.

What happened in the districts that got everyone through quality training as quickly as possible? They "checked the box," and then everyone went back to work. Little, if anything, changed.

What I learned from that experience fundamentally shaped my approach to strategic change, and it provided the foundation for my consulting practice and many more successes over the next 20 years.

In short, what I learned was that it takes ruthless consistency to drive strategic change.

WHAT RUTHLESS CONSISTENCY DOES *NOT* MEAN

I want to make sure there's no misunderstanding. To some, the concept of ruthless consistency might come across as inflexible, regimented, or limiting. Where is there space for creativity and innovation if the objective is to do the same things the same way all the time? As Oscar Wilde once remarked, "Consistency is the hallmark of the unimaginative."

Let's be clear. Ruthless consistency does *not* mean robotic repetition. It's *not* about mindless and mechanical activity performed without variation simply for the sake of being consistent. I'm *not* suggesting we become technocrats and submit to the tyranny of consistency.

What I am championing is a *ruthless consistency of purpose*, one that is constantly projected in your decisions and your actions. Because the relentless alignment of intentions, decisions, and actions is the foundation of success. That is a fundamental truth.

Ruthless consistency means that everything you do—*as creative and innovative as that might be*—is consistently aligned with your purpose, your intentions. Ruthless consistency not only allows for creativity and innovation, it demands it. Why? You're operating in an ever-changing environment. New technologies emerge. Customers' needs change. Processes become obsolete. Practices get stale. What made your organization successful in the past could kill it in the future. Creativity and innovation are *requirements* of ruthless consistency, not enemies.

> The relentless alignment of intentions, decisions, and actions is the foundation of success.

And don't mistake "ruthless" as implying a cold-hearted or cruel approach to strategic change, one that views people as mere objects of production. What it implies is *an uncompromising commitment* to your stated purpose. Fulfilling that commitment requires you to understand, encourage, and reinforce the human spirit, not squash it.

Make no apologies for ruthless consistency. It doesn't mean being inflexible or inhuman. It means being committed and effective.

TAKEAWAYS

- What matters more than anything you do is *everything* you do. Doing something could be worse than doing nothing, because misaligning anything could undermine everything.

- Be ruthlessly consistent. Develop the right focus. Create the right environment. Build the right team.

MAKE IT HAPPEN

All the models, forms, and questionnaires in this book can be accessed at: RuthlessConsistency.com by entering the password: MakeItHappen.

2

SECOND PRINCIPLE
What You Do Is Not as Important as What *Your People* Experience

If you think you're leading, but no one is following,
then you're only taking a walk.

—John Maxwell

"I CAN'T BELIEVE IT!" The CEO was visibly upset. "How can our employees rate us so poorly?" The employee survey results had come back, and the ratings for "Communications" were not good. Items such as "Upper management communicates the company vision and strategy" and "Upper management updates us on company performance" scored especially low. "We've had meetings, we started a newsletter . . . we've told them!"

I wasn't surprised. I'd seen this movie many times. Leader thinks he does a good job communicating. Employees think otherwise. Leader concludes that communications aren't the problem; employees are the problem.

Reframe your thinking. It doesn't matter that you're *telling* if they're not *hearing*. Just like it doesn't matter that you're training if they're not learning, or that you're empowering them if they don't feel empowered. What matters is what *they* perceive, what *they* believe, and what *they* feel. Why? They're the ones doing the real work. They're providing the service; they're making the product; they're engaging the customer. Implementing strategic change depends on *them*.

> *What matters is what* they *perceive,*
> *what* they *believe, and what* they *feel.*

Remember the first principle of ruthless consistency? What's more important than anything you do is *everything* you do. We need to build on that. Second principle: What you do is not as important as what *your people* experience. Ultimately, it's not about you. It's about them.

MIXED MESSAGES KILL CREDIBILITY

You think you're being consistent. *They* think you're sending mixed messages.

Take the case of a national sales director in the telecom industry. Her boss approached her with a project he called a "triple-A1" priority. It *had* to get done, and it had to get done *now*. What could be clearer than that? Not so fast. It turns out that *every* request he made was a triple-A1 priority. Everything had to get done now.

Her reaction?

"It was never clear what was or wasn't a top priority. It was frustrating. Basically, I just worked on what I thought was most important. Some of those triple-A1 priorities didn't get done. But I don't know if he noticed or cared, or if it even made a difference."

When you *say* everything is a top priority, what people *hear* is nothing is a top priority. You're sending a mixed message. So what did the national sales director think about her boss?

"I don't think he knew what he was doing. And that wasn't just my view. People stopped taking him seriously. His triple-A1 priorities became a running joke in our company."

Now consider the case of a call-center customer service rep. He enjoyed solving customers' problems and took pride in creating a positive call experience. That was aligned with his company's stated commitment to providing the best customer service in the industry. But things weren't what they appeared.

"At first I believed all the marketing propaganda—that the company really did care about providing great service. But it was bull. All management cared about was productivity—how many calls you processed and how quickly you got through each call. It was demotivating. I felt like they lied to us."

And what did frontline management think?

"Look, I know we talk 'service,'" said one manager, "but the reality is that I'm evaluated on labor costs and productivity—calls per FTE [full-time-equivalent employee] and average call time. My bonus is tied to that. Sure, upper management talks the talk about customer service, but at the end of the day all that matters to them is the dollars."

Mixed messages. Misalignment. Inconsistency. Do you see the effect it has on people?

Beware. Everything you say and everything you do sends a message. When you send mixed messages, you confuse people, you demotivate them, and you kill your credibility—and you're probably not even aware of it. When you trumpet excellence yet tolerate poor performance, you're sending a mixed message. When you tell people they're empowered yet punish them for making bad decisions, you're sending a mixed message. When you invest in technology yet don't provide training and support, you're sending a mixed message. The messages you send had better be consistent. Or else.

> *When you send mixed messages*
> *you confuse people, demotivate them,*
> *and kill your credibility.*

Once you've killed your credibility you're in big trouble because they stop listening to you—and even if they listen, they don't believe what you're saying is real. Why should they get on board with the new SCI when they don't believe that *you're* on board, that *you'll* follow through? Is it any wonder that many employees' reaction to management's latest, greatest SCI is, "Let's batten down the hatches until this blows over"?

What's especially tragic is that mixed messages massively deflate your top performers, the ones most driven to succeed, the ones who desperately want a strong, focused, and consistent leader. When you fail to live up to that, you puncture their spirit.

THE PSYCHOLOGY OF INCONSISTENCY

People are bloodhounds for inconsistency. The moment you say one thing but do another—boom!—they're on it. That's how we're wired from the time we're young. Ever have a child point out when what you did wasn't consistent with what you said?

"Why did you do that when you told me not to?"

"Uhhhhh . . ."

And if you used that lame do-as-I-say-not-as-I-do justification, you'd have only made it worse.

Inconsistency captures our attention in a way that consistency does not. Consistency is assumed; it's expected. When that expectation is violated, alarm bells go off.

> *People are bloodhounds for inconsistency.*

Make no mistake. You are constantly on stage. Your employees are watching and judging your every move. They read meaning into everything you say and everything you do. Every decision, every action, every gesture, every expression, every word . . . everything. They also read meaning into everything you *don't* say and *don't* do—like when you don't recognize someone who puts in extra effort or when you don't provide them with the resources to get the job done.

When your words and actions are in conflict, which do you think they believe? Right. Your actions. That's why it's critical you consistently *role model* the values and behaviors you want them to model. If you want people to act with respect, then always be respectful. If you want a culture in which people reliably meet commitments, then be impeccable in meeting your commitments. Effective leaders know that role modeling is more powerful than telling.

What makes all of this so challenging is that it takes only one slip-up. One inconsistent act. Promote product quality a hundred times yet ignore poor quality just once, and which will they remember? Emphasize "team first" yet just one time act selfishly, and which will they think is the real you? There are no take-backs. A single inconsistent act and your credibility is suspect or, worse, ruined.

THE CULT OF LEADERSHIP

To be fair, we haven't been trained to view the world from our employees' perspective. We've been trained to view it from a leader's perspective. Countless books have been written, presentations delivered, and workshops conducted on leadership: what great leaders do; how great leaders became great leaders; how you, too, can become a great leader.

Yet if there's one thing I would sear into your mind about leadership, it's this: *It's not about you. It's through you.* What you do is validated only by what *they* experience and, as a consequence, what *they* do.

For people to do what you need them to do and perform at their best, first you have to understand their perspective. Ultimately, this is about empathy. *Seeing through their eyes. Thinking in their minds. Feeling with their hearts.* And then taking the right actions.

Many years ago, I came across a book entitled *The Platinum Rule*.[1] An alternative to the Golden Rule—do unto others as you would have them do unto you—the Platinum Rule states, *Do unto others as they would have done unto them.* Exactly. What drives your actions shouldn't simply be what *you* would want so much as what *they* would want. And don't assume that all your team members want the same thing—they don't. Some need you to point them in the right direction and then get out of the way. Others need you to reinforce every step they take, so they feel secure taking the next one.

> *Empathy is seeing through their eyes, thinking in their minds, and feeling with their hearts.*

We consider individual differences when it comes to our customers. One customer likes basketball, so we give her tickets to a basketball game. Another enjoys plays, so we give him tickets to the theater. When we're intentional, we can empathize with others. So why not with our people?

It's natural to lionize successful leaders. Yet, ultimately, being a successful leader is not about what you do. It's about what your people experience.

THE SECRET TO BUILDING A HIGHLY ENGAGED, HIGH-PERFORMING ORGANIZATION

For over 20 years, *Fortune* magazine has published an annual edition, "The 100 Best Companies to Work For." Each year, *Fortune's* research partner—Great Place to Work—surveys millions of employees across more than 50 countries to assess their work experience.

Recently, when Great Place to Work decided to reanalyze the results from past winners, it made a troubling discovery: A company could make the 100 Best list yet have "major disparities among the experiences of frontline employees."[2] Those disparities were masked when a company's results were averaged out. It turns out that some of the best companies to work for were not great places to work *for all*.

As a result, Great Place to Work revised its analysis methodology so that "higher expectations will be placed on each company to ensure that employees' experiences are consistent . . . a standard we refer to as a 'Great Workplace for All.'"[3] Consistency. More important than what the average employee experiences some of the time is what *every* employee experiences *all* of the time.

This isn't just about being a great place to work. This is about *business performance*. The companies that rated highest as a result of the new methodology grew revenues *three times faster* than their competitors.[4] Clearly, the consistency of employees' experiences helps drive *both* engagement and performance.

TAKEAWAYS

- What you do is not as important as what *your people* experience.

- When they perceive you sending mixed messages, it confuses them, demotivates them, and kills your credibility.

- To drive engagement and performance, create a consistent experience from *their* perspective.

- It's not about you; it's through you.

3

THIRD PRINCIPLE
You're Not as Committed as You Need to Be . . . Yet

> *You don't get 100 percent results with only 50 percent commitment.*
>
> —Anonymous

HOW COMMITTED ARE YOU to winning?*

It's a question I've asked thousands of leaders at the start of my presentations.

"One hundred percent!" "Totally committed!" "I'm all in!"

Everyone's confident; everyone's committed. Or so they say. When I ask them again at the end of the presentation, the bravado is gone. There's an uncomfortable realization they haven't been as committed as they thought they were—or need to be.

Good. Now they're ready to change.

---

*I use "winning" as a metaphor for "success," for achieving your goals. It doesn't mean there has to be a "loser."

WHAT'S MORE IMPORTANT
THAN THE WILL TO WIN

I want to test your commitment. I want *you* to test your commitment. Because it's one thing to *say* you're committed and another to *be* committed.

Think of a failed SCI you've experienced. Now, write down all the reasons why it failed. (Stop. Seriously, stop. Take two minutes to do this.)

(Were you *committed* enough to take the two minutes? Or did you automatically jump to this paragraph? I thought so. If you haven't done it yet, take the two minutes now.)

Now, be brutally honest. Were *you* as committed as you needed to be to successfully execute that SCI?

Did you set specific goals? Did you regularly communicate them throughout your organization? Did you communicate *why* you needed to achieve them and *how* you intended to achieve them? Did you cascade the goals down the org chart? Translate them into individual expectations? Adjust your measurement and reporting systems to stay focused on them?

Did you provide your people with the knowledge and skills needed to achieve the goals? With sufficient resources—materials, budget, and time? With sufficient authority to make decisions and take action in support of the goals?

Did you provide them with ongoing feedback and guidance about their performance? Did you recognize and reinforce them for the right behaviors and right outcomes? Did you hold them constructively accountable when needed?

Did you redesign whichever processes needed to be redesigned in support of the goals? Revise whichever policies needed to be revised? Change your org structure as required? Invest in the necessary infrastructure—facilities, equipment, and systems?

Did you revamp your recruitment process to attract the people who could best help you achieve the goals? Ensure your selection process enabled you to reliably select the best candidates?

Were you committed enough to identify, examine, and align *every touchpoint* with your goals, so as to overwhelmingly tilt the odds in your favor? Did you persevere when the change wasn't happening or wasn't happening quickly enough? Did you determine why it wasn't happening and what *you* needed to do differently to make it happen?

Were you committed enough to deal with the inevitable, ongoing, and myriad work pressures, aside from the SCI, without caving on your commitment?

Now, with all of this in mind, how committed were you to winning?

Commitment is best summed up by what I heard a famous football coach say many years ago: *"There's a big difference between the will to win and the will to do what it takes to win."* Exactly. And you'd better understand that difference. Many of us have the will to win. We love the feeling of winning. We want to be associated with winners. But do we have the will *to do what it takes* to win?

> There's a big difference between the will to win and the will to do what it takes to win.

IT'S ABOUT TO GET UNCOMFORTABLE

True commitment comes at a price.

Lindsey Vonn was willing to pay that price. Vonn is the most accomplished female ski racer in history. Over an unparalleled,

18-year career, she won 82 races, 8 World Cup downhill (season) titles, 5 super-G titles, 4 overall World Cup titles, and an Olympic gold medal. Wow! Yet what those numbers don't speak to was *the intensity of her commitment*.

As a young child, Vonn was not particularly coordinated or physically gifted. Sports, it seemed, was not where Vonn would make her mark. Yet she possessed two crucial traits that formed the bedrock of her future success. She was very observant, always watching others to see what worked, what didn't, and why. And she was willing to work harder—much, much harder—than anyone else.

By her own estimation, Vonn skied *tens of thousands* more slalom gates than any other young skier in the United States. And once she made it to the World Cup circuit, her commitment didn't wane. She turned heads early on with her famously wicked training schedule. Vonn would train six hours a day, five to six days per week, year-round—far more than anyone else on the circuit—to improve her strength, agility, and endurance. Her personal trainer never had to push her to train. He had to push her to not *overtrain*.

But that was just one part of the formula. The science of physical training dictates that major exertion demands major recovery. Vonn's recovery schedule included 10 hours of sleep *and* a 1-hour nap each day.

Her relentless desire to improve was also reflected in her approach to the technical side of the sport. For many years, she was the only woman on the US ski team who recorded how her equipment performed in testing. She came up with the idea of having a sports scientist shoot ultrahigh-speed video of her skiing to better understand the interactive effect of snow conditions and various equipment combinations on performance. She trained extensively with the Norwegian men's ski team—which included the top two male skiers in the world—so she could study their dynamics and ski lines. All of this with the goal of finding the hundredths of seconds that can make the difference between success and failure.

Are you getting a sense of what true commitment looks like?

There's more.

There's fighting through unexpected setbacks with the unwavering resolve to come back even stronger. In Vonn's case, that included ruptured knee ligaments, knee fractures, a badly splintered humerus bone, related nerve damage, a broken ankle, broken fingers, concussions, and what doctors initially feared was a broken back.

There's more still.

There's making a conscious choice *not* to do all those things you *want* to do because they would keep you from doing the things you *have* to do. From her early years through to adulthood, Vonn recalls missing out on school dances, sleepovers, friendships, fun events, weekend getaways, vacations, and just having a somewhat normal social life.

True commitment comes at a price. That's what got Lindsey Vonn to the top. But—and this is important—her goal was not just to *get* to the top; it was to win more ski races than any woman ever had, than any person ever had. So her regimen remained her regimen *even when she was at the top of her sport*. No complacency, no letting up. Total commitment. Ultimately, when the cumulative effect of injuries finally forced her to retire, Vonn's 82 race wins were 20 more than that of the previous women's record holder, Annemarie Moser-Pröll, and only 4 short of tying the men's record holder, Ingemar Stenmark.

To be committed, you don't have to be a world-best skier whose training routine borders on maniacal, who suffers broken body parts, or who misses out on all the things you don't want to miss out on. But don't thump your chest and trumpet how committed you are when you've done only a small fraction of what's possible.

> *Don't thump your chest and trumpet how committed you are when you've done only a small fraction of what's possible.*

A COMMITMENT CASE STUDY

A highly successful, mid-market company that likes to fly under the radar—let's call it SuccessCo—has over the past 50 years become one of the largest real estate development and management companies in its state.

The company's story is one of both evolution and reinvention. Originally a contracting company, SuccessCo expanded into various segments of the construction industry until it concentrated its focus on developing and managing commercial real estate and residential apartment communities. Over time, it became known for operational excellence, won multiple Workplace Excellence awards, and continually placed at or near the top of industry rankings for residential satisfaction. Its exceptional financial performance reflected all of that.

But that wasn't good enough. SuccessCo's Executive Team understood how easy it would be for complacency to set in and for the company to lose its edge. They determined that while operational excellence was important, it was even more important that the company develop a *culture of innovation*, one in which employees would be empowered to continually try new things to drive improvement and results.

Committed to achieving this, they assembled a guiding team—sponsored by an Executive Team member—to define, promote, enable, and support the desired culture. It was at this point that the Executive Sponsor—let's call her Jada—asked me to help them structure the initiative, challenge their assumptions, and guide the journey.

Our first task was to select members of the guiding team, which we called the Innovation Team. It would have been easy to simply select people from different functions or locations to ensure we had appropriate "representation." Instead, our priority was to select people who had the right *traits and skills* to be highly effective contributors: people who saw possibilities not just problems, who were doers not just talkers, who had strong interpersonal skills, and who were respected by their peers.

With the Innovation Team in place, we established a charter that outlined our purpose, objectives, goals, branding, roles, and team norms. We then developed an *Operational Framework* for submitting, evaluating, implementing, and tracking ideas. We wanted processes that were simple and easy, yet would give us the data we needed to learn and evolve. We created a *Marketing Framework* for communicating and promoting the initiative, and for recognizing and celebrating progress and success. We developed a *Support Framework* to make sure that every employee touchpoint, everything that shaped *their* experience, was consistently aligned with our objectives. To oversee our efforts, we established a *Management Framework* that outlined how and when the Innovation Team would meet to track progress, assess the three other frameworks, and make necessary revisions.

Before launching any of this, we conducted a *minesweeping* exercise by asking ourselves the question, "Why will this fail?" Anticipating what could cause the SCI to fail allowed us to identify preventive and corrective actions.

Instituting these frameworks, our focus in the first year was to create an environment that would educate and encourage employees, and have them feel comfortable submitting ideas. We wanted to build a habit of generating and submitting ideas, and create an expectation that this was the norm. One incentive that generated buzz was the offer to give every employee a week off at the end of the year if, collectively, they submitted over 100 ideas. At the same time, we set a target of implementing a modest number of improvements (25) in that first year.

What happened? As Jada observed, "There was a pent-up desire to improve things that employees saw needed improving. Over 150 ideas were submitted, and almost a third were implemented. We made tremendous progress that first year and saw evidence of real cultural change. Not only did people start *thinking* about how the business could be improved; they would approach their managers with their ideas. Managers were more open and responsive to those ideas. And everyone *saw* ideas being implemented. All of that told us the culture was starting to change."

The Innovation Team played a key role in enabling the change, helping employees to craft and refine their ideas, coaching managers on how to constructively engage employees who approached them with ideas, and continually massaging ideas through to implementation when warranted. It was a good start, but only a start.

We discovered that some employees were reluctant to propose ideas that involved spending money. Those who received bonuses based on financial performance were naturally risk-averse. For others, it was simply the fear of feeling responsible for spending money that might not result in anything.

So the company upped its commitment. It not only budgeted $150,000 for the implementation of innovation ideas; it *mandated* that that money had to be spent in year two *regardless of the certainty of the outcome*. And spending the $150,000 would have no negative effect on bonuses. The only requirement was that each idea should reasonably be expected to have some impact on operational performance, the customer experience, employee engagement, or financial results. The message was that experimentation and innovation had to become part of the culture. Commit to the process, learn from the process, and the results will follow.

Removing the disincentives to spend money on innovation allowed employees the freedom to experiment and to learn. They discussed what worked, what didn't, and why. Not only was the money spent, but we saw an increasing number of tangible improvements.

The process evolved. We created a category of ideas called "Just Do It!" that didn't need to be submitted or evaluated; employees could simply act on them. Still, we kept track of those ideas so we could understand what was being done, what resulted, and how the culture was changing.

We actively sought input from employees about how to evolve the initiative. If the goal was to develop a culture of innovation, then we, the Innovation Team, needed to role model innovation in our efforts.

The following year, another $150,000 was allocated as must-spend for implementing innovation ideas. The year after that, it was upped to $300,000. Momentum grew, the results kept building, and the new culture took root. Innovation became a normal part of how SuccessCo did business. And, yes, the financial results justified the investment.

Why did this approach succeed while so many others fail?

"We approached it as a system," said Jada, "a system focused on people. We took a comprehensive approach, so that everything was consistent with what we wanted to achieve. It wasn't just a project.

"It's important to be flexible and adjust as you go, and to listen to everyone involved. These initiatives have to evolve organically. They can't just be top-down.

"We've seen a lot of improvements in the customer experience, employee experience, operations, and our financial results. But the biggest benefit is that we now have a culture where every employee is empowered to try new things. It's super energizing. And having this kind of culture helps us attract and retain quality employees."

Commitment. It's not about holding motivational launch meetings, making big sweeping gestures, or pushing people through training. Pull back the curtain on any successful SCI and you'll see a commitment that's reflected in all the arrows pointed continuously in the right direction. You'll see ruthless consistency.

You can't be kind of, sort of, somewhat committed. If you are, you'll fail. It takes intense commitment. The journey won't be easy. Doing what it takes to win involves sacrifice. Often, you'll feel uncomfortable. That's how it's supposed to feel.

How committed are you to winning? Your move.

TAKEAWAYS

- You're not as committed as you need to be . . . *yet*. And unless you up your commitment, your SCIs will fail.

- Determine what your organization needs to achieve. Determine the level of commitment needed to make it happen. Then ask yourself, "Am I willing *to do what it takes to win?*"

PART II

THE RIGHT FOCUS

One thing must not be forgotten. Forget all else, but remember this, and you'll have no regrets. Remember and be concerned with everything else, but ignore this one thing, and you'll have done nothing. It is as if a king has sent you on a mission to a foreign land to perform one specific task for him. If you do a hundred things, but not this appointed task, what have you accomplished?

—Rumi

It starts with the right focus. A focus that articulates, *"What* must we achieve? *Why* must we achieve it? *How* will we achieve it?" Without a concise "what," there is no focus. Without a compelling "why," SCIs are merely should-dos, not must-dos. And without a clear "how," the "what" is nothing more than a dream.

You're committed to winning? Then start by developing the right focus.

Ruthless Consistency®

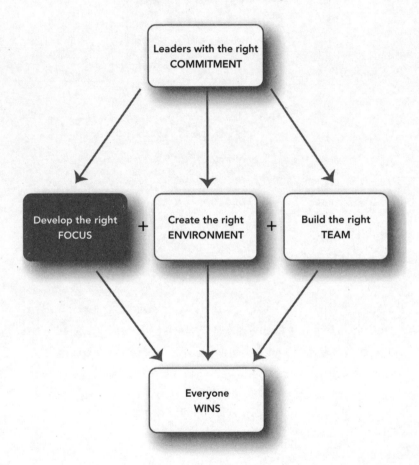

Leaders with the right
COMMITMENT

Develop the right
FOCUS

+

Create the right
ENVIRONMENT

+

Build the right
TEAM

Everyone
WINS

4

STOP STRATEGIC PLANNING

Without strategy, execution is aimless. Without execution, strategy is useless.

—Morris Chang

I'VE SURVEYED THOUSANDS of business leaders—CEOs, business owners, and Strategic Leadership Team members—asking them the question, "In your experience, do strategic change initiatives more often fail because of poor planning or poor execution?" Almost everyone says, "Poor execution." Of course. We have good ideas, good intentions, and maybe even good plans . . . but execution is where they so often fail.

There are few better examples than the annual strategic planning charade. Remember the failure rate noted in the Introduction? Between 70 and 90 percent. Why? The most common reason is that once we've developed the plan, we fall back into the clutches of day-to-day demands. We lose focus. Execution bogs down.

Jay Dargatz, the CEO of a restoration company, describes it this way: "After the strategic offsite meeting we would come back all guns blazing . . . at least for the first couple of months. But then people got busy with their work, and we'd lose momentum. We weren't consistent with our updates, and we didn't set specific timelines or deadlines. And looking back, we should have held people more accountable.

"I don't think everyone understood the consequences of not executing our strategies. It didn't help that the process was so top-down. We just didn't involve enough people—or enough people from different levels—at different stages of the process. We didn't translate the strategy so that it was meaningful to everyone. As a result, I think people felt it was something we were doing to them instead of with them."

Any of that sound familiar? There has to be a better way.

There is.

THE STRATEGIC MANAGEMENT PROCESS

When you read "strategic planning," what comes to mind? The off-site meetings? The plan? Strategic planning emphasizes the wrong thing: the *planning*.

Stop strategic planning. To develop *and sustain* the right focus, strategy has to be a *process*, not just an event. The goal isn't just to *develop* a plan or even *implement* a plan. The goal is to *institute a system* that ensures strategy is an ongoing, managed process.

> *Strategic planning emphasizes the wrong thing: the planning.*

The *Strategic Management Process* has four phases: *Assess, Position, Plan,* and *Implement*.

Strategic Management Process

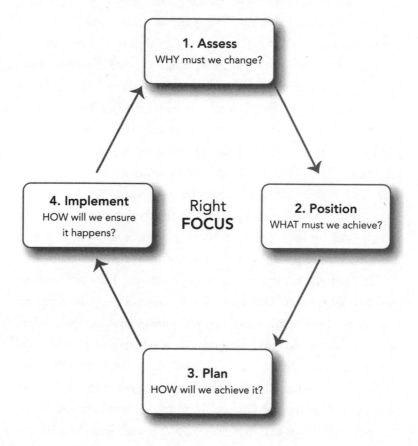

In the *Assess* phase you develop a compelling *Case for Change*—the strategic "why." It emerges from a solid understanding of the strategic context in which your organization operates, context that spotlights *gain* and *pain*—the consequences of changing versus not changing. Chapter 5 expands on how to create a compelling Case for Change.

In the *Position* phase you concisely define your strategic positioning—the strategic "what." What are we driven to achieve, what business are we in, what makes us desirably different in the marketplace, and what must our culture look like to win? Chapter 6 outlines what good strategic positioning statements look like and how to avoid the failings of the typical mission and vision statements.

In the *Plan* phase you clearly outline the critical few SCIs that must be accomplished for your organization to win—the strategic "how." This phase charts the course from strategy to reality. Chapter 7 explains why most plans are designed to fail, how focusing on your value proposition could destroy your business, and why you shouldn't pursue a sustainable competitive advantage. It also describes how to prioritize and select the most essential SCIs.

The outputs from the Assess, Position, and Plan phases capture the why, what, and how of your strategy—your *Strategic Framework*. However, it's meaningless unless you vigorously undertake the fourth phase—*Implement*. In the Implement phase you sustain focus by: (1) *instituting mechanisms* to systematically manage implementation, (2) *creating an environment* that consistently points people in the right direction, and (3) *securing the capabilities* that can and will make it happen. Chapter 8, and then Parts III and IV, detail how to do this.

How does strategic management stand apart from strategic planning? In short, strategic management is *strategy + execution*. The following table captures the main differences:

Strategic Planning	Strategic Management
An event	A process
Creates focus	Creates and sustains focus
Periodic	Continual
Generates a plan	Generates a plan, action, and results
Leaders delegate execution	Leaders actively oversee execution

A STRATEGIC MANAGEMENT CASE STUDY: NORTH AMERICAN TEA & COFFEE

Riyaz Devji had had enough. As the CEO of North American Tea & Coffee (NATC), a manufacturer and distributor of private label food products, he was tired of poor financial results, high employee turnover, and ongoing customer complaints. He was sick of workdays spent mired in the details of the business, instead of overseeing the business. When I first met him, it was clear he was committed to change. He was ready for strategic management.

1. Assess

Working with NATC's Strategic Leadership Team, our first step was to comprehensively assess the current situation, starting with NATC's customers. To get a range of perspectives, we conducted surveys of their customers' buyers and category managers, as well as interviews with their directors. The results were not good, which surprised the NATC Strategic Leadership Team. Many directors and category managers rated NATC poorly as a strategic partner, saying it didn't have a good understanding of their business and priorities, and didn't offer ways to better support them. All customer groups had serious concerns about packaging quality, fill rate, and on-time delivery. The results were not all bad, however, as NATC's people were rated as both professional and personable.

We also conducted interviews with 17 key suppliers to determine their perceptions of NATC and identify how NATC could become a better partner. The conclusion: NATC was an unremarkable customer that elicited mildly favorable impressions.

Analyzing NATC's financial performance painted a more worrisome picture: Revenues were highly concentrated in one client, and overall margin and EBITDA performance was poor, especially in one of the company's two major locations.

We conducted an anonymous survey of NATC's 250 associates to gain their perspectives about immediate supervisors, upper management, the work environment, and the culture. While the results were generally good, they also exposed areas of concern: Training was lacking. Managers did a poor job of engaging, communicating with, and supporting associates. Incentives and rewards were not well aligned with performance expectations. In short, NATC had not created an environment that enabled people to perform at their best.

The Case for Change emerged: If NATC didn't become a strategic partner to its major customers, understanding their priorities and reliably meeting their needs, it would be at risk of losing those customers, which would be disastrous. If it didn't become financially viable in its underperforming location, it would be forced to restructure. And if it didn't create an engaging environment for its associates, then performance and results would both suffer. On the other hand, doing these would solidify customer relationships, build a more engaged and high-performing team, and significantly improve financial results.

2. Position

Next, we established NATC's strategic *positioning,* starting with a *Brand Commitment* statement: "Trusted Partner • Great Service • Fair Prices." We also developed a simple *Winning* statement: "Profitable . . . with happy customers, associates, and suppliers." That led us to construct a *Strategic Scorecard* with associated metrics and goals.

3. Plan

In the *Plan* phase, we identified three critical objectives: (1) We must become a strategic partner to our major customers, (2) we must ensure our underperforming location becomes financially viable, and (3) we must create an environment that effectively engages our associates.

In support of the first objective, we identified two SCIs. The first was to develop and implement a rigorous CRM system, committing to specific, customer engagement and reporting requirements. The second was to implement a customer-centric, quality measurement system with metrics and goals for packaging quality, fill rate, and on-time delivery.

For the second objective, we identified several smaller initiatives, including assessing and reducing material cost structure, bringing product blending in-house for high-volume brands, and developing new product variations for quick release-to-market. To meet our third objective, the primary SCI was to develop an engagement-performance system with key elements including communications, training, performance coaching, and reinforcement.

So far, so good. But up to this point, all we had was a plan. Now we needed to turn strategy into an *ongoing, managed process.*

4. Implement

The critical first step in this phase was to engage all the associates (within each geographic location) in an interactive *One Team Meeting*. The Strategic Leadership Team presented the Strategic Framework, and then we asked the associates—seated at round tables with flip charts—to discuss what they liked about it, what concerned them, and what questions they had. At each table, one associate recorded comments, and one reported out highlights to the larger group. The discussions were vigorous. Everyone had a voice. And we took away many helpful ideas. The associates' post-event feedback verified that the One Team Meeting was an enlightening and energizing event.

However, if we didn't continue to communicate about progress and success, then we risked squandering momentum. To avoid this, we implemented an ongoing, multichannel Communications Plan with clear objectives, timelines, and responsibilities.

To drive implementation, we identified a *Champion* for each SCI. The Champions created *Execution Plans* for their respective SCIs, identifying team members, time-linked milestones, resource requirements, and the projected return on strategy. We held monthly *Progress Tracking* meetings to monitor progress of the Execution Plans and review our Strategic Scorecard. We also conducted a midyear *Recalibration* meeting with the Strategic Leadership Team to determine what if any adjustments we needed to make to the Strategic Framework and Strategic Management Process. As a result, we revised one of the Execution Plans and enhanced our Communications Plan, increasing upper management's involvement in recognizing and celebrating successes.

Unsurprisingly, this comprehensive approach led to comprehensive results. Key performance indicators such as packaging quality, fill rate, and on-time delivery all improved. The culture began to change, morale rose, and associate retention increased. NATC became viewed as more of a trusted partner to its major customers. EBITDA increased by 50 percent in less than two years, and the growth in associates' profit-sharing checks reinforced their efforts. An unanticipated benefit was that Devji found he was spending less than half the time he used to spend fighting fires. He was able to devote more time to working *on* the business instead of *in* the business. Shortly thereafter, he sold his company to a private equity firm for a strong multiple.

"No question," said Devji, "Committing to strategic management was the single best investment of time and money I made as a CEO."

Don't just plan strategy, manage it. Put an end to the strategic planning charade. Commit to strategic management.

TAKEAWAYS

- Planning is important, but the goal isn't to create a plan. The goal is to develop and sustain a compelling, concise, and clear focus, effectively execute on it, and be able to do it repeatedly.

- Stop strategic planning. Commit to strategic management.

5

EMBRACE THE JOY OF PAIN

Nothing so concentrates the mind as the sight of the gallows.

—Samuel Johnson

WHAT DRIVES AN ORGANIZATION to change? We have intentions and visions and big, audacious goals, yet for most organizations these aren't what reliably predict change. Having a *psychologically compelling reason to change* is.

TWO FUNDAMENTAL DRIVERS OF CHANGE

In simple terms, there are two fundamental drivers of change: the drive to achieve and the drive to avoid. While the outcome of these drivers may be tangible or intangible, rational or emotional, the motivation basically boils down to gain and pain.

Much has been written about the first motive, the drive to achieve. The importance of having a vision, a big, audacious goal,

Strategic Management Process

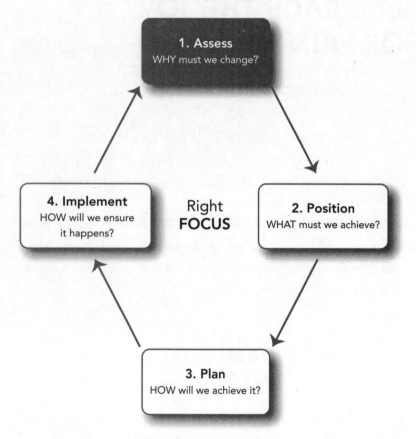

is something we're reminded of constantly. And some highly motivated and visionary leaders have led their organizations to great heights based purely on the drive to achieve. But they're the exception.

Organizations are far more likely to change when they have a strong drive to achieve a desirable outcome, *coupled with* a strong drive to avoid an undesirable outcome. Much less has been written about the drive to avoid, yet it's generally the more powerful drive. Evidence of this is found in the work of Nobel Prize–winner Daniel Kahneman, a pioneer in the field of behavioral economics whom I studied with while completing my PhD. It turns out that the pain associated with a prospective negative event is more intense than the gain associated with a prospective positive event *of the same magnitude.*[1] For example, the prospect of reducing your salary by 20 percent feels worse than the prospect of raising your salary by 20 percent feels good. Cognitive biases like this influence our decision making, including decisions about whether or not to change.

> What drives an organization to change is having a psychologically compelling reason to change.

Pain and gain—each can be motivating yet, combined, they create a psychologically compelling Case for Change.

FOUR POISONS THAT KEEP YOUR ORGANIZATION FROM CHANGING

Organizations don't change because they don't feel compelled to change even if they know they *should* change. Why?

Complacency. Complacency is the narcotic that dulls the drive for change. It enters your organization's veins through the needle of success. The symptoms? Blindness to emerging threats, hardening of attitudes, softening of performance standards, and dulled reactions. When complacency takes hold, your organization drifts into that comfortable state of "good enough."

Arrogance. Similar to complacency, but with an extra shot of ego. The smug feeling that you're better and smarter than your competitors, that you've figured it out, and that you've got the results to prove it. If you're at the top of your game, then why change?

The fallacy of extrapolation. This is the stubbornly persistent yet mistaken belief that present trends will continue into the future. Your organization is performing well, so of course it will continue to perform well. Why wouldn't it? Any evidence to the contrary is written off as a blip.

Psychological inertia. This is the natural tendency to keep doing what you've been doing the way you've been doing it. It's efficient. Over time, you develop patterns and you don't question them or even think about them. They become habits.

How many of these poisons have seeped into your organization? Before charting your strategic course, you need to make sure your Case for Change—gain and pain—is powerful enough to overcome complacency, arrogance, the fallacy of extrapolation, and psychological inertia.

Where to start? Find the pain.

THREE WAYS TO FIND THE PAIN

The joy of pain is that it helps drive your organization to change by providing an antidote to the four poisons. Here's how to find it:

1. It Finds You

Cognac became a revelation in the late sixteenth century. An enterprising Dutch captain determined that by distilling the town of Cognac's much-prized white wine, he could transport twice the quantity to Amsterdam. There, it could be reconstituted with water. Yet when the people of Amsterdam tasted the fine, distilled beverage, they recoiled at the thought of adding water. Cognac, the drink we know today, was born.

By the mid-1800s, the town of Cognac was thriving. Its eponymous spirit was in high demand throughout Europe, trade was strong, money was flowing, and stock levels were high. What could possibly go wrong?

What could go wrong was the accidental import of a tiny, aphidlike vine louse from the New World—*phylloxera vastatrix*. It spread unchecked through the vineyards of Europe, feeding on the roots of vines and reproducing rapidly in great numbers. The effect was devastating. Some estimates suggest that 90 percent of all European vineyards were destroyed. The Cognac trade was decimated.

Sometimes, the pain finds you. And when it does, it creates an immediate and compelling Case for Change. *Something has to be done.*

In the case of Cognac, many solutions were attempted, but to no avail. French grape growers even took to burying a live toad under each vine to draw out the "poison." Nothing could slow the scourge. Finally, it was discovered that grafting indigenous grape vines onto phylloxera-resistant rootstock from the New World yielded a robust vine that didn't compromise the flavor of the grapes. It took five years of lab research to find a rootstock variety that was best suited to the *terroir* of Cognac. Eventually, it was found . . . in Denison, Texas. The Cognac industry was saved.

(*Side note:* As the import of Cognac slowed to a trickle, British drinkers were forced to turn to a local product that distillers and blenders had finally developed to a high standard. Scotch.)[2]

The benefit of pain finding you is that it forces you to change. You can't ignore it; you can't rationalize it away. You have to take action. Or else.

2. Anticipate It

Your organization isn't experiencing any pain? Then you'd better anticipate it.

The second most popular team sport in the world is not baseball, not rugby, not basketball, and not hockey. It's a 400-year-old sport: cricket. In the early 2000s, cricket wasn't in pain, but there were warning signs. Attendance was down, sponsorship had slipped, and there didn't seem to be the same number of young people taking to the sport. Was this a blip or something more significant?

The England and Wales Cricket Board (ECB) decided to take account. While the premise of the game was still compelling, the format increasingly wasn't. One-day cricket matches last eight hours. "Test cricket"—considered the game's highest standard—

has matches that can last up to five days. In an accelerating world, that format is hardly conducive to TV viewership, fan commitment, or even a casual outing. The warning signs didn't seem like a blip; they seemed like a trend.

Confirming their insights with market research, the ECB did something courageous and dramatic. It designed a new variation of the sport: Twenty20. Lasting roughly three hours, Twenty20—or T20 as it's popularly known—was intended to supplement, not replace, test cricket. What happened? First officially played in 2003, T20 skyrocketed in popularity. Today, there are national leagues, international competitions, world championships, and TV rights worth billions of dollars. T20 is now the most watched form of cricket worldwide. And test cricket? Numerous articles have been written about its slow demise and pending death.

The ECB anticipated the pain and took bold and decisive action. Take a walk through the graveyard of organizations that didn't. Thomas Cook Travel Group knew what its customers wanted for 178 years—until it didn't. The same was true for "The Greatest Show on Earth"—Ringling Bros. and Barnum & Bailey Circus (over 140 years). Blockbuster, Motorola, Toys "R" Us, Borders Books . . . the headstones extend as far as the eye can see.

Anticipate the pain you will experience if you don't change. How do you do that? By *attacking your assumptions*.

Assumptions can be grouped into three categories: market assumptions, internal assumptions, and macro assumptions.

Market Assumptions

Market assumptions refer to your (current and potential) target market segments, customers, competitors, and suppliers. Here are two of the most common market assumptions you're likely to make:

Assumption: Our Customers Love Us!

Yes, and every once-successful, now-deceased company was able to say the same thing. It doesn't matter that your customers loved you yesterday or love you today. The world evolves; things change. Customer satisfaction does not equal customer loyalty! What customers are loyal to is *value*. The moment they think someone else just might be able to provide better value than you is the moment they're ripe to leave.

Assumption: We're Better Than Our Competitors

Which competitors? Your current ones or the ones who haven't yet emerged, who are looking to disrupt your industry, and who can bring superior resources and change the game? And what makes you so sure you're better than your current competitors? Or that they're standing still? When you underestimate your competitors, you become vulnerable.

Internal Assumptions

Internal assumptions relate to your products, services, processes, structure, people, and systems. Here's an assumption almost every company makes:

Assumption: We Have Great People

Maybe. Yet how do you validate that? Even if your people are better, how do you know they're consistently *performing* better than your competitors or that you'll be able to retain them? And once you assume your people are superior, you're likely to become lax about performance standards.

Macro Assumptions

Macro assumptions refer to the *STEEP* factors—the sociocultural, technological, economic, environmental, and political factors that could put your business out of business. Recall how the accelerating pace of society (a sociocultural factor) severely threatened the future of cricket, and how a tiny vine louse (an environmental factor) all but decimated the cognac industry. Here's a macro assumption we've seen play out more than once:

Assumption: The Economy Is Growing So It Will Keep Growing
The problem is that the economy often doesn't provide a lot of advance warning before it starts slowing down. Even when the warning signs appear, are you usually too quick or too slow to react? Think subprime lending crisis or global pandemic. If you're too exposed, and don't protect your company against the next, inevitable downturn, then you could become a casualty of economic Darwinism.

Attack your assumptions. Market assumptions, internal assumptions, and macro assumptions. It's an effective way of anticipating the pain that could threaten your business.

3. Create It

If the pain hasn't found you and if there's no plausible pain to anticipate, then as a last resort you have to create it.

That's what Yvon Chouinard did. Chouinard is the founder of Patagonia, the outdoor, high-performance clothing retailer with a strong environmental focus. Patagonia was a successful company with a well-established brand, innovative and fashionable product lines, deep-rooted relationships, and solid financials. In short, no pain.

When an internal analysis revealed that the most environmentally damaging fiber Patagonia used was industrial-grown cotton, Chouinard decided to create the pain. He gave the company 18 months to stop using it. Period. How significant was that? At the time, 25 percent of Patagonia's $250 million business was based on products made with industrial cotton!

What happened? The prospective pain of losing more than $60 million in revenues was simply unacceptable. The company made the switch within 18 months. Its stand on using only environmentally friendly cotton resonated with the market, helped to further differentiate and elevate its brand, and made it an even more profitable business.

Pain—recognize it, anticipate it, create it. It's the most effective antidote to the four poisons that keep your organization from changing.

THE SOLUTION: DEVELOP A COMPELLING CASE FOR CHANGE

Your objective in the Assess phase is to attack your assumptions, understand the strategic context in which your business operates, and develop a Case for Change—the strategic "why." It must be compelling enough to overcome the four poisons that inhibit organizational change, and it should take into account the two fundamental drivers of change—pain and gain.

Here are examples of paired Case for Change statements developed with our clients:

If we don't optimize our product portfolio, then revenues and margins will continue to shrink, and our future will be at risk. (pain)

If we optimize our product portfolio, then revenues and margins will grow, which will help secure our future. (gain)

If we don't adopt and utilize targeted technologies, then we will continue to lose customers and new customer opportunities. (pain)

If we adopt and utilize targeted technologies, then we will gain relevance and recapture customers and market share. (gain)

If we don't attract and hire the right people, then growth will cause us to implode. (pain)

If we attract and hire the right people, then we will have the capabilities to support growth. (gain)

How many paired Case for Change statements should you have? As few as one, but no more than five. Too many will dilute your focus.

With a well-thought-out Case for Change, it becomes almost unthinkable that you wouldn't take action. Each pair of statements offers you and your Strategic Leadership Team a stark choice. Pain or gain. Your choices will determine your legacy. Choose well.

TAKEAWAYS

- The two fundamental drivers of organizational change are pain and gain.

- Complacency, arrogance, the fallacy of extrapolation, and psychological inertia each inhibit organizational change.

- The best way to overcome these inhibitors is to recognize, anticipate, or create the pain of not changing.

- Develop a compelling Case for Change—the prospective pain of an undesirable outcome *coupled with* the prospective gain of a desirable outcome.

CLIMB THE RIGHT MOUNTAIN

Follow your heart, but take your brain with you.

—Alfred Adler

YOU'RE CLEAR ABOUT WHY your organization needs to change. Now, what would it look like for your organization to "win"?

OUR BIG, AUDACIOUS GOAL

When I was young and foolish, my buddy Ken and I decided to test our rock-climbing skills on Cascade Mountain in the Canadian Rockies. Having done almost no research, we arrived at the mountain, picked out a route that looked promising, and began to climb. Without ropes, of course.

It was all going well. Until it wasn't. The climbing got increasingly difficult, and we soon realized we were at the limit of our abil-

Strategic Management Process

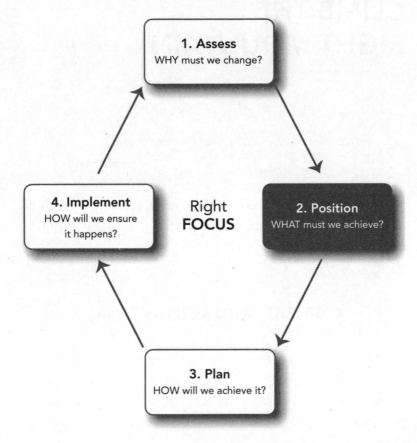

1. Assess
WHY must we change?

2. Position
WHAT must we achieve?

3. Plan
HOW will we achieve it?

4. Implement
HOW will we ensure
it happens?

Right
FOCUS

ities—and our risk tolerance. Just one problem: We now had to downclimb. Hmmm, hadn't planned for that.

We quickly learned one of the fundamental truths of rock climbing: Climbing down is a lot harder than climbing up. At one point, still high on the rock face, Ken couldn't find the next move down and his legs started shaking from fatigue. "I don't think I can hang on," he yelled, his voice cracking. This, at the exact moment I was 20 feet *directly below him* on the rock face. Which meant if he were to fall, he would crash into me and send us both plummeting off the mountain and into the obituaries section of the annual alpine journal.

Fortunately, Ken was able to steady himself and find the next move. With considerable anxiety, we continued, and finally were able to downclimb to the base. At which point, we noticed the memorial plaques bolted to the rock wall for climbers who had lost their lives there.

The point? We had a big, audacious goal. It's easy to set a big, audacious goal. But if you're not clear on the *implications* of pursuing it, then what you aspire to could destroy you.

You'd better understand why.

THE THREE Rs: REWARDS, RISKS, AND REQUIREMENTS

Dream big! Develop a vision! Follow your passion!

And why not? We're continually inspired by stories of those who had big dreams and the motivation, courage, and persistence to fulfill them. The entrepreneurial spirit in all its glory!

Yet the more common stories, the ones you're less likely to read about, are of those who pursued big dreams, and failed. You don't see book titles trumpeting *Broken Dreams: How I Pursued My Passion, Failed Miserably, and Lost Everything*.

You're not going to like what you're about to read next, but it's the truth.

An unfortunate consequence of the popular view that you should dream big and pursue your passion is that it implies *any* dream is worth pursuing.

It isn't.

Not every dream is worth pursuing? Don't pursue your passion? What kind of negative, self-defeating advice is that?

Stay with me. I'm not saying you shouldn't dream big. I'm saying that *before you commit* to pursuing your dream, you need to understand the three Rs—rewards, risks, and requirements. Understanding these allows you to answer the question, "Is this a dream I am truly committed to pursuing or not?" There's no wrong answer, as long as it's an informed answer.

Once you conjure up your next big dream, ask yourself these questions:

"Why that dream? Why not some other dream?"

"What rewards make it uniquely worth pursuing?"

"What risks and consequences are associated with pursuing it? Am I willing to accept them?"

"What is required to fulfill the dream? Am I willing to meet those requirements?"

> Before pursuing your dream, understand the three Rs—rewards, risks, and requirements.

For some organizations, the dream is an arbitrary number: *Grow to $100 million in sales within two years.* OK, but why that number (other than the obvious reason that it's a round number)? Why not $75 million? Why not $125 million? Why not $91.6 million? What *rewards* make that number uniquely worth pursuing? Is there anything of significance other than hitting a round number? Is that compelling in and of itself?

What *risks* are associated with growing to $100 million in sales within two years? Could growing quickly cause you to outstrip your infrastructure? Could your ability to deliver on time slip? Could your customer service suffer? Could decision-making get bogged down? How likely are those possibilities? What are the consequences, and are you willing to accept them? Could you and would you act to mitigate them?

What is *required* to fulfill the dream? Would it force you to make acquisitions? Would it mean taking on debt and increasing your exposure? Would it mean giving up equity? Are you willing to meet those requirements to realize the dream?

Some might say that asking questions like these can suck the heart and soul out of a dream, that subjecting our dreams to the filters of reason would result in many dreams never being pursued and many successes never being achieved. I would say that *not* asking these questions can result in you discovering too late that you're climbing a mountain you don't want to be on.

Why do successful companies fail? Research suggests that two of the most common reasons are (1) they get caught up in the *undisciplined pursuit of more,* and (2) they *deny the risks and perils* associated with their decisions.[1] The first occurs when growth becomes *the sole purpose* of a business, instead of *the outcome* of a purposeful and well-designed business. The second occurs when leaders fall victim to the illusion of infallibility.

Knowing what you now know, are you comfortable with dreaming big and following your passion *without* asking yourself about rewards, risks, and requirements?

There's nothing wrong with dreaming big, wanting to climb a rock wall, or becoming a $100 million company. Just make sure that the rewards are compelling, that you understand and are willing to accept the risks, and that you recognize and are willing to meet the requirements.

Don't let reason *dictate* which dreams you pursue. But don't pursue your dreams *ignoring* the voice of reason.

> *Don't let reason* dictate *which dreams you pursue. But don't pursue your dreams* ignoring *the voice of reason.*

MISSION FORGETTABLE

How do you capture your ambition in words? For many organizations, it's the *mission statement*. If you have one and can automatically recite it, then congratulations. If you're like most leaders, you either struggle with or don't remember your mission statement. And if it's supposed to be *the* most important statement about your organization, then what does that say about you? Or the mission statement?

We'll talk about you later. Let's say the problem is with your mission statement. Pull up a chair; get comfortable. One of our clients had the following mission statement (I've removed references to the company name and industry to protect it from much justified embarrassment):

At (company name) we seek to be the best (industry) company in town as viewed by our customers, employees, and competition. We are a customer-oriented and profit-motivated (industry) company that offers a quality product with excellent service and differentiates itself from its competitors as the best not the biggest. We are a company that does not overreact to market conditions or competitor actions, nor are we strangled by cost control measures; instead, we monitor critical expense areas to ensure bottom line success. We also pride ourselves on our reliability, and we constantly strive to improve the quality of life for our employees—our greatest asset.

We want to be a company that:

- Is built on relationships with long-term customers—in fact, we consider our customers as our partners in success

- Provides quality service which allows us to grow

- Interacts with our customers and welcomes their feedback

- Does everything we can to not only assure a pleasant experience for our customers but to exceed their expectations

- Pays attention to our people, training them to be more effective and better equipped to serve our customers

- Looks for change in all areas and makes it a driving force

- Is technologically progressive

- Recognizes our civic responsibility, which is not only our obligation but which is just good business

- Has a spirit of entrepreneurship that comes from seeing ourselves as a partner with our clients—when they do well because of our service, we will do well

Over 240 words! How can you possibly create focus and alignment around a 240-word mission statement? The number one problem with many so-called mission statements is that they're simply too long. They don't create focus, people don't remember them, and they don't lead to action.

Even if they're not too long, many mission statements suffer from being too cliché: "High quality ... blah, blah, blah ... superior value ... blah, blah, blah ... customer focus ... blah, blah, blah ... trust ... blah, blah, blah."

There's nothing wrong with quality and value and customers and trust. Yet statements that include all of these come across as reciting the obvious, as true but hollow. Are they supposed to distinguish you from the companies that stand for low quality, inferior value, customer indifference, and deceit?

There's little consistency in how mission statements are used. I've seen them used as declarations of intent, as tag lines, as descriptions of a business's offerings, as statements of what makes a business unique, or as affirmations of some underlying purpose. One outcome of this fuzziness is the ongoing debate about what is a mission and what is a vision. While some might argue there's a clear distinction between the two, the reality is that vision statements are used in as many different ways as, and often interchangeably with, mission statements.

The result is that in the past 25 years the usage of mission and vision statements has dropped from a high of 88 percent, when they were *the* most popular management tool, to 32 percent.[2]

That may not be a bad thing, because employees today are becoming increasingly cynical about mission statements. They don't want interminable statements, they don't want tired clichés, and they're not interested in semantic debates about what is a mission and what is a vision.

I'm no longer a fan of the traditional mission and vision statements. Yet to develop and sustain focus, it's critical you establish your *strategic positioning*.

FOUR STRATEGIC POSITIONING QUESTIONS YOU MUST ANSWER

Answering the four strategic positioning questions establishes the core of your strategy. It then shapes everything you do.

1. What Business Are We In? (What We Do)

Imagine I meet you for the first time and find out you work for ABC Company. What's the universal question I ask you?

"What do you do?" Meaning, what does your company do? Do you have a concise, consistent, coherent answer to that question? If you're fumbling and stumbling, trying to come up with the right words, then I'm not impressed. Not good.

Let's assume you do have a concise, coherent answer. If I then meet someone else from your organization and ask her to remind me what your company does, her answer had better be the same as yours. Otherwise, I'm going to be confused, and I'll think your company is confused. Not good.

A core part of your strategic positioning is being absolutely clear about what business you're in. The statement that captures this is called the *What We Do* statement. Here's an example:

"We help people by restoring buildings and possessions that have been damaged by fire or water."

Clearly, this is a restoration company. I have a basic understanding of what the company does (restores buildings and possessions), what leads the company to do it (fire or water damage), and what the company's purpose is in doing it (helping people). I now have a basic understanding of its business. Notice that it's not simply, "We help people," which, although purposeful, is too general and doesn't make clear what business the company is or is not in. Does it help people by taking them grocery shopping? By walking their dogs? By providing financial advice? Notice also that it's not a sexy statement or a noble statement. Yet I didn't ask for sexy or noble. I simply wanted to know what your company does. That's why it's called the What We Do statement.

Here's another example. We worked with a region of the National Kidney Foundation (NKF). The NKF offers or supports a number of services related to kidney health and disease, including research, education, prevention, and treatment. The region's statement describing what it does was comprehensive, accurate, and entirely forgettable. Instead, we wanted a statement that was memorable and would engage people to find out more. Working with the regional leadership, here's what we came up with:

"We help people pee."

That was it. Easy to understand, easy to remember, and, yes, it was very engaging. We sponsored 5k walk/run events and had T-shirts made up that proudly proclaimed, "We help people pee!" It was just cheeky enough that people would chuckle and then ask us about it. That was the goal.

Note that the statement has only one more word than "We help people," which I said is too general. Adding *what* we help people do provides just enough specificity.

What makes a good What We Do statement? Four criteria:

- Easy to understand—simple, not too conceptual

- Not too general, not too specific—conveys the basic purpose of the business

- Easy to remember—fewer than 20 words

- Engaging—creates the "pull" for follow-up questions

Everyone on your team needs to know what game you're in and what game you're *not* in. That's captured in the What We Do statement.

2. What Are We Driven to Achieve? (Winning)

A *Winning* statement describes what success looks like and answers the question: What are we driven to achieve? It's future-oriented. It avoids the semantic mission versus vision debate. And it doesn't mean there has to be a *loser*. It's about your organization—what *you* aspire to achieve.

What should winning look like? Growth? Imagine that you've led a company for seven years, and that during your tenure revenues have fallen by 14 percent, unit sales by 8 percent, and market share by 9 percent. Imagine that major publications have written about what you've done to the company.

Is that winning?

In the case of Alan Mulally, former CEO of Ford, it was. He was heralded as the star among CEOs of US auto manufacturers because despite the dramatic decline in key result metrics, during the same period Ford went from an annual loss of $12.6 billion to a profit of $7.2 billion. Share price increased by 90 percent. Mulally's *strategic focus* was to create a much more profitable Ford, which meant becoming a smaller company. He succeeded.

Attack your assumptions. Winning doesn't necessarily mean growing revenues, becoming a bigger company, or capturing more market share. Don't confuse results with strategic results.

OK, but we should always focus on growing profit, right?

Not so fast. Think of Amazon. For many years, Amazon was unprofitable or, at best, marginally profitable. Yet profitability wasn't its focus. Its focus was to capture market share, dominate online retail sales, and become synonymous with e-commerce. Accomplishing that was costly. It required access to an almost limitless range of products, reliable and timely distribution, and hard-to-match pricing. Once that was achieved, and once Amazon expanded the monetization of its services through Amazon Prime memberships, profitability skyrocketed. Again, don't confuse results with strategic results.

But shouldn't we always want to grow?

Yes, you should always want to grow . . . stronger. Grow stronger in pursuit of what you're driven to achieve. Grow stronger so you can fend off competitors, win customers, exploit opportunities, and overcome threats. Grow stronger by evolving your offerings, improving your processes, developing your people, and providing more value to your customers. If you're going to focus on one thing that you should always grow, it's stronger.

Then how do we determine what winning looks like?

Sometimes, your Case for Change points the way. For example:

"If we don't release a compelling upgrade to our flagship product within 12 months, then customer defections will accelerate and our financial position will become unsustainable.

"If we release a compelling upgrade to our flagship product within 12 months, then we will reestablish ourselves as industry leaders, recapture lost customers, and entice new customers."

In this example, when a company was on the brink of collapse, winning was very targeted: Ensure sustainability by releasing a compelling product upgrade within 12 months.

Other times, it might simply be that you, the leader, have a clear picture of winning and are intensely driven to achieve it. Here's an example of one ambitious young CEO's Winning statement:

"We will become the de facto standard for interactive TV worldwide."

Still other times, you and your Strategic Leadership Team might craft a Winning statement. Here's an example of a team-crafted Winning statement:

"Feeding the passion of quilters and sewers better than anyone else."

This company distributes quilting and sewing products and is focused on creating "pull" for those products through retail outlets. In this case, winning is ongoing. It's not associated with a fixed time, as in the first example, or a specific outcome, as in the second example.

Notice that in only one of the above statements is winning tied to a number (the compelling product upgrade needs to get to market within 12 months). Yet every Winning statement should have quantitative *metrics and goals* associated with it. After all, having a Winning statement is meaningless unless you measure progress and success. For example, "Feeding the passion of quilters and sewers better than anyone else" could be measured by comparative market-share numbers or comparative end-user satisfaction ratings.

What makes a good Winning statement? Here are five criteria to keep in mind:

- Future-focused—what the organization aspires to achieve

- Easy to understand—simple, not too conceptual

- Easy to remember—fewer than 20 words

- Measurable—so you can evaluate progress and success

- Inspirational—evokes a positive emotional response

To develop and sustain focus, you need to be clear about what you're driven to achieve—what winning looks like.

3. What Makes Us Desirably Different? (Brand Commitment)

Whether you're leading a business or some other type of organization, you're undoubtedly faced with competition. Someone else is offering what you're offering to the same market segments. So how will you compete and win?

In the marketing world, people talk about differentiation. How do you stand out from your competitors? Yet that misses the point. You could be different and *irrelevant*. Different in a way that nobody cares about or likes. The goal isn't to be different; it's to be *desirably different*. Who gets to decide? Not you. You need to be desirably different *in the eyes of your target market segments*.

If your brand is what others think and feel about you, then what do you want them to think and feel? That's your *Brand Commitment*. As an example, here is the Brand Commitment of a company that designs and administers retirement plans:

"To be the most trusted name in retirement plan servicing"

Trusted by whom? Banks, investment advisors, third-party administrators, and others. By living that Brand Commitment, their belief is that client acquisition and retention will follow.

Another client, a faith-based school, identified three pillars as central to its Brand Commitment:

Outstanding Education • Spiritual Foundation •
Confidence and Social Skills

Consistently delivering on those three pillars will help the school positively impact young lives and attract more students and more funding.

As with the Winning statement, metrics and goals should be attached to your Brand Commitment. If you want to be "the most trusted name in retirement plan servicing," you can determine that through customer and market research. If you want to provide an "outstanding education, spiritual foundation, and confidence and social skills," you can determine that through graduation rates, comparative rankings, university acceptance levels, test results, behavioral metrics, and self-reporting.

Don't worry if your competitors claim to have a similar Brand Commitment. Ultimately, it's not about who can *claim* to be desirably different; it's about who can *execute* on being desirably different.

Why do I use the term "Brand Commitment" instead of the more popular "brand promise"? Simply because it conveys a stronger sense of, well, commitment.

What makes a good Brand Commitment statement? It should meet these five criteria:

• Easy to understand—simple, not too conceptual

• Easy to remember—fewer than 20 words

- Functional—when well executed, makes you desirably different

- Measurable—so you can evaluate how well you're living up to it

- Engaging—creates the "pull" for follow-up questions

You have to compete to win. Determine how you can be desirably different. That's why you need a Brand Commitment.

4. What Must Our Culture Look Like to Win? (Cultural Commitments)

The final element of your strategic positioning speaks to your culture—the kind of culture that is fulfilling, that makes people feel like they belong, and that enables them to live your Brand Commitment and to win. The spirit of this is captured in your *Cultural Commitments*.

What does that look like? A client in the insurance industry decided the single most important element of a winning culture is caring—everyone in their company needs to deeply care. Here are the company's Cultural Commitments:

WE CARE

About our colleagues, clients, carriers, company, and community

Mutual respect

Integrity

Accountability

Professionalism

Passion/Fun

When your overarching Cultural Commitment is "caring," it needs to be a touchstone for who qualifies and does not qualify to be a part of your organization. It should determine the behaviors you promote, the actions you reinforce, and the practices you institute.

Once you've identified your Cultural Commitments, you must treat them as inviolable, not simply as cultural nice-to-dos. Few things in an organization inspire as much cynicism as hollow statements about culture or values, words on the wall mocked by behaviors between the walls.

The moment of truth comes when a top performer violates one of your Cultural Commitments. What do you do when that happens? I guarantee that if you overlook the behavior, tolerating it because the person is a top performer, you'll demotivate everyone else and completely discredit your Cultural Commitments. On the other hand, if you act deliberately, constructively confronting the person's behavior regardless of how good a performer he is, you'll raise morale and reinforce those commitments.

When people feel they belong to an organization that is truly aligned with their identity—who they believe themselves to be or who they aspire to be—it elevates their spirit and deepens their commitment. That's why Cultural Commitments are critical.

BUT WHAT ABOUT "PURPOSE"?

Isn't there something missing? Doesn't having a sense of purpose provide the inspiration and meaning that keeps work from being, well, just work? Shouldn't that be captured in a *Purpose* statement?

Yes, a sense of purpose is vitally important, but that doesn't necessarily mean you need a stand-alone Purpose statement. Purpose can be embodied in your What We Do statement. Do you remember, "We help people by restoring buildings and possessions that have been damaged by fire or water"? That reflects a sense of purpose along with describing what the company does. A previous version began, "We restore buildings and . . ." Sure, that described what they do, but there was no sense of purpose.

Purpose can also be embodied in your Winning statement: "Feeding the passion of quilters and sewers better than anyone else." That reflects a sense of purpose, along with winning.

Sometimes, however, you may want to highlight purpose in a stand-along Purpose statement. That was the case with a company that provides healthcare professionals with orthopedic and rehab solutions. Its Purpose statement: "We help people move and live better!"

Once you've answered the four strategic positioning questions, then decide. Do you need a stand-alone Purpose statement, or is it well captured in one of your other statements?

TAKEAWAYS

- Before committing to a big, audacious goal, make sure the *rewards* are compelling, the *risks* are worth taking, and you're willing to meet the *requirements*.

- Answer the four strategic positioning questions. Get clear about what business you're in (and not in), what you're driven to achieve, what makes your organization desirably different, and what your culture must look like to win.

DO LESS, USE MORE RESOURCES . . . NO, REALLY

It's not the notes you play, it's the notes you don't play.
—Miles Davis

YOU'VE IDENTIFIED *WHY YOU* need to change. You've determined *what* you need to achieve. Now, you need to plan *how*. How are you going to realize the gain and avoid the pain outlined in your Case for Change? How are you going to win? How are you going to live up to your Brand Commitment and Cultural Commitments?

Through your strategic change initiatives, your SCIs.

IDENTIFYING POTENTIAL SCIS: WHAT TO CONSIDER

How do you identify potential SCIs? Your Case for Change and Strategic Positioning statements will point you in the general direction. Still, there are many potential SCIs you could take on.

Strategic Management Process

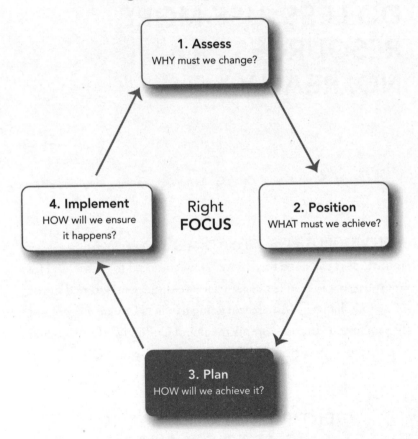

When identifying potential SCIs, many organizations think of established principles of strategy, such as "develop a strong value proposition," "differentiate yourself," or "identify a sustainable competitive advantage," Yet each of them could send you down the wrong path.

A Strong Value Proposition Could Destroy You

It's natural to start with your value proposition, determining how to compete and win in the marketplace. Unfortunately, a strong value proposition alone could destroy your business. Successful strategy depends on the alignment of three propositions: (1) your *value proposition*—how you attract, secure, and retain customers; (2) your *people proposition*—how you attract, engage, and retain the right people who can deliver on your value proposition; and (3) your *financial proposition*—how you organize and model your business to generate a sufficient financial return.[1]

Think of Uber: a compelling value proposition with a suspect financial proposition. People love the convenience . . . but companies that lose billions of dollars each year don't make it in the long run. Will Uber be able to develop a compelling financial proposition before it's too late?

Even if you have a compelling value proposition and a strong financial proposition, a weak people proposition could undercut your business. Struggling to attract or keep the talent you need could cause your growing business to implode.

When you're considering potential SCIs, make sure to consider all three propositions.

When to Be Just like Your Competitors

You want SCIs that help make you desirably different, but that's not the whole story. For some things, it's important to be the same as your competitors. If your organization is weak in areas where your competitors are strong, and if customers view those as must-haves, then being desirably different in other areas won't make up for it. For example, if you have the best product, but you can't reliably deliver it on time, then you've got a problem. If you offer a service that wows customers, but it's hit-or-miss depending on which team member is providing it, then, again, you've got a problem.

You have to play defense as well as offense. Sometimes, you need to take on SCIs that shore up deficiencies. So, yes, there are situations when you should be the same as your competitors. Because as important as it is to be desirably different, it's just as important *not* to be undesirably different.

Descend to Summit

It's tempting to buy into the *Grand Illusion of Business*: continuous, straight-line growth—and the belief that every SCI should support continuous growth.

In the real world, successful businesses often follow "S-curves." They periodically reinvest, retrench, or reposition for the *next* growth opportunity. In the short term, the financials might take a hit, but that might be acceptable because what's more important than growth in the next quarter is *to lay the foundation for growth* into the future. Geographic expansion, new systems, enhanced facilities, research and development—there are many strategic reasons to invest *even if that hinders short-term results*.

It's like climbing a mountain. Naturally, you want every step to take you higher on the mountain. Yet, as in business, the terrain sometimes dictates that you have to descend into a gully before you get to the summit. When you're climbing at altitude, fighting for air and taking multiple breaths for each step, the last thing you want to do is give up hard-won elevation by descending and then have to regain it. It's counterintuitive; it can be psychologically deflating. But sometimes there is no other way.

Strategy is about identifying what you need to do—as difficult and counterintuitive as that might be—to get to where you need. Sometimes you have to descend to summit.

The Myth of a Sustainable Competitive Advantage

It's one of the most accepted truisms of business strategy: You should pursue a *sustainable competitive advantage*. It could be a unique business model, a proprietary technology, dominant branding, or any number of things. Attaining a sustainable competitive advantage is the gold standard of strategy.

It's a lie.

There is no such thing as a *sustainable* competitive advantage. BlackBerry didn't have it. Kodak didn't have it. Blockbuster didn't have it. And the 178-year-old Thomas Cook Travel Group didn't have it. Yet at one time, all of them clearly *had* competitive advantages.

Help me out here. Exactly which companies have a *sustainable* competitive advantage?

There is no such thing. How could there be? Evolving markets, changing social norms, emerging technologies—*the entire context within which any business operates is constantly changing.*

If you pursue a sustainable competitive advantage, you're likely to overlook the very thing that strategy requires: *continually creating temporary competitive advantages knowing that they're temporary.* Why? Because the only safe assumption you can make in business is that any advantage you have will be copied, leapfrogged, or made obsolete.

What's worse is if you think you have a sustainable competitive advantage. Because then you get complacent, maybe even arrogant. You take your foot off the gas. You become vulnerable.

Some people resist the idea that there is no sustainable competitive advantage. I've heard people argue that *continuous innovation* is the one, true, sustainable competitive advantage. Sorry to disappoint you. Your innovations could be met with confusion or, worse, yawns in the marketplace. I'm sure you remember Clairol's Touch of Yogurt shampoo, Burger King's Satisfries, Harley-Davidson perfumes, and Cheetos Lip Balm, right?

Don't take this to mean you shouldn't innovate. You absolutely should innovate. Because even though innovation doesn't guarantee success, failing to innovate all but guarantees failure.

Forget *sustainable*. Pursue and keep pursuing *temporary competitive advantages*.

> *If you think you have a sustainable competitive advantage, you take your foot off the gas and you become vulnerable.*

Be a Cannibal

Don't be reluctant to pursue promising opportunities—new products, services, market segments, or channels—*even though they might cannibalize your current revenues.* Because if you're thinking of those promising opportunities, you can be sure that others are, too.

Netflix intentionally and aggressively pursued video on demand through a separate business unit, knowing it would cannibalize its legacy DVD rental business. Blockbuster, on the other hand, was reluctant to act on and slow to pursue the same opportunity. We know how that movie ended.

Count on this: If you choose *not* to cannibalize your revenues, then your competitors will eat you alive. *Bon appétit.*

PRIORITIZE YOUR PRIORITIES

No matter how much I warn you, you're still going to fall into the trap. You're going to take on too many SCIs because you're ambitious, you see the opportunities, and like the proverbial kid in a candy shop, you grab at everything. What happens? Resources get diluted, people get stretched too thin, and before you know it, instead of everything being a priority, nothing is a priority. Failure.

Cody Sudmeier, a client who has run several successful companies, described it this way: "Our strategy sessions always led us to take on more. More opportunities, more activities, and, ultimately, more distractions. The more we took on, the less we got accomplished. It was only when we decided to focus on what mattered most, what was absolutely essential to our success, that we were able to reinvent our business and reinvigorate our financial growth."

Do less; do less; do less. Stop trying to do it all. You can't do it all. Not all at once. Concentrate your focus. Concentrate your resources on what matters most. Doing less allows you to apply more resources (as needed) to the top priorities. Do less, and you'll accomplish more. As Tim Cook, CEO of Apple, once explained, "We say no to great ideas in order to keep the amount of things we focus on very small so we can put enormous energy behind them."[2]

How many is too many? A $20 million company asked me to review their one-year strategic plan. Incredibly, it had over 40 SCIs! Yes, that would be too many. Generally, you should take on no more than three; depending on their scope and complexity, you could take on up to five. But if you do, elevate one of those initiatives as the must-do, no-excuses, this-will-get-done-or-else initiative.

When the term "investment guru" gets thrown around, Warren Buffett is the name referenced more than any other. Yet, what many don't know is that one of Buffett's greatest strengths is his ability to prioritize, to do less.

His personal airplane pilot once came to him for career advice. Buffett asked him to go through a three-step exercise:

Step 1. Write down your top 25 career goals.

Step 2. Circle your top 5 goals.

Step 3. Look at the list of 20 goals you *didn't* circle.

In Buffett's words, "Everything you didn't circle just became your Avoid-at-All-Cost list. No matter what, these things get no attention from you until you've succeeded with your top 5."[3]

Exactly. It's not the obvious non-priorities you need to fear. It's the *almost* top priorities. Because their appeal will diffuse your focus, deflect your attention, and divert your time.

The same is true of strategy. Everything can't be a triple-A1 priority. Strategy is just as much about what you choose *not* to do as it is about what you choose to do. Focusing on the few allows you to concentrate your resources, time, and energy on what's most important.

> *It's not the obvious nonpriorities you need
> to fear. It's the almost top priorities.*

Let's say you've come up with a list of potential SCIs. How do you prioritize them? You could conduct or contract out in-depth research into each option. Then you could make well-informed decisions. However, for many mid-market companies, conducting or contracting out in-depth research isn't practical.

Another approach would be for your Strategic Leadership Team to simply debate the various options. Yet debating options often isn't the best way of making decisions. Because the person who prevails is sometimes the one who has the most forceful voice, or the most authority, or who is willing to argue the longest. What gets sacrificed is an objective and open-minded assessment of the various options.

There's a better way.

What works well in practice for mid-market companies is an approach more practical than extensive research, yet more structured than simply debating options:

1. Conduct targeted research into the most promising SCIs.

2. Identify criteria for evaluating the relative merits of each, such as:

   - Resource requirements

   - Length of time to complete

   - Payback timeline

   - Organizational trauma

- Probability of success

- Return on investment

- Consequences of failure

- Overall impact on winning

3. Determine if any criteria should be weighted and if any should be immediate disqualifiers.

4. Discuss and rate each potential SCI against each criterion (using, for example, a 1–5 scale); total the ratings.

5. Compare the overall ratings for each option and ask if they pass the "gut test." Does your assessment of their relative merits seem fair and reasonable?

6. If yes, select the very few top-rated items that the organization has the means to strongly support. You've prioritized your priorities. If no, then revise the evaluation model and go through the first five steps again.

Is this process somewhat subjective? Sure. Is that OK? Yes. While some might say that objective data should drive every decision, the reality is that we can make good decisions using both "Is"—information and intuition. Yet be careful. While intuition can be rooted in subconscious knowledge resulting from experience and deep insights, it can also be unreliable. Many successful visionaries have been guided by their intuition, but many *unsuccessful* visionaries—the ones you never read about—have also been guided by intuition. Still, all things considered, intuition should at least have a seat at the decision-making table.

Make decisions using both "Is"—information and intuition.

Does everyone on your Strategic Leadership Team have to agree on the priorities? No. Don't be held hostage by strict consensus. Strict consensus means that anyone who disagrees has the power to veto. Not good. At the same time, be leery about making decisions based on a simple majority. It could leave many team members uninspired. For major decisions, it's best to achieve a critical mass of those who agree (at least two-thirds), as long as the others can live with and support the decision.

Keep in mind that not *every* strategic decision needs to be a Strategic Leadership Team decision. There *are* times for autocratic decision-making, when you as the leader should decide. And there are times when your team members simply want *you* to make a decision, so they can get on with it. Endless discussion or perceived indecisiveness can be demoralizing. There are times when you as the leader need to lead.

TAKEAWAYS

- Beware that a strong value proposition, focusing exclusively on differentiation, insisting on continuous growth, pursuing a sustainable competitive advantage, and avoiding cannibalization could each destroy your business.

- Do less! Prioritize your priorities, concentrate your resources, and you'll accomplish more.

PUT THE "EXEC" IN EXECUTE

The leader sees leadership as responsibility rather than as rank and privilege.

—Peter Drucker

YOU'VE DEVELOPED A *Strategic Framework*. You've got a compelling *why*, a concise *what*, and a clear *how*. Now comes the hard part—making it happen. That doesn't mean you and the Strategic Leadership Team have to do all the work, but it does mean that you have to *own* it. You can't just develop strategy and hand it off to others, hoping it will get done. That's not being strategic. That's being lazy.

CLEAR YOUR PLATE

Everyone's energized. You've come out of your annual strategy session with a clear focus and a set direction. But then reality starts to seep in. Your plate is already overflowing. How are you going to find the time to get it all done?

Strategic Management Process

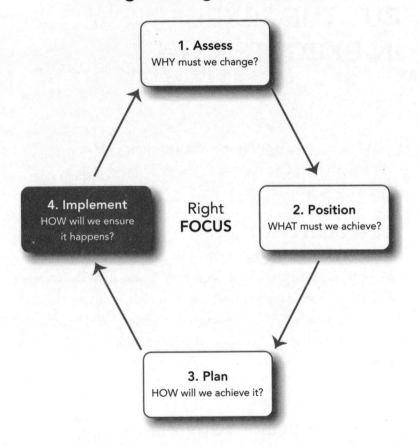

Clear your plate. All of us spend time on activities that, if we're honest, add little or no value. Eliminating those activities allows us to free up time for the strategic work. The first thing to do after developing your Strategic Framework is to take your Strategic Leadership Team through a "clear your plate" exercise.

Have each Strategic Leadership Team member list all the meetings they attend, processes they're involved in, reports they review, and tasks they regularly perform. Next, have them take a scalpel to that list, cutting away anything that truly isn't adding value. Anything that can be eliminated, shortened, scaled back, streamlined, or off-loaded. Estimate and then annualize the total time savings across the entire team. Finally, attach a dollar value to the total time saved based on the average, all-in compensation for a Strategic Leadership Team member.

You will be shocked at the dollar value of the time spent that's *not adding value*. All those little things that, repeated again and again, become a *big* thing—a big waste of time. When we go through this exercise with Strategic Leadership Teams in mid-market companies, the dollar value of the time saved can be up to $80,000 per year.

MINESWEEPING: THE ONE QUESTION YOU SHOULD ALWAYS ASK

Now that your team members have cleared their plates of nonessential activity, ask them this one question about each SCI: *"Why will this fail?"*

Conduct a "minesweeping" exercise and have them list all the reasons your SCIs could fail. Encourage them to consider the factors that caused past SCIs to fail including self-defeating management practices, weak processes, and cultural misalignments. Then discuss these as a team, with you speaking first to role-model that it's safe to talk about them. Make sure to take responsibility for what you didn't do but should have done and what you did do but shouldn't have done. That will give them the courage to speak their own uncomfortable truths. When they do, recognize and reinforce them for their courage.

Once you've identified what could cause an SCI to fail, determine what *preventive* actions you need to take as well as *corrective* actions if the SCI starts to go off the rails. For example, one of our clients, a retailer of luxury products, determined that one reason its Customer Experience SCI could fail was if service staff didn't understand the difference between good service and outstanding service. At the time, the service staff believed they were providing outstanding service. To show what outstanding service looked like, managers took staff members to select restaurants, hotels, and other venues known for outstanding service so they could experience it firsthand. The intention was to overcome any misunderstanding by highlighting the gap between good and outstanding. The corrective action was to institute weekly debrief sessions in which staff members would discuss recent service scenarios and provide feedback and suggestions to each other about what they could have done differently to deliver outstanding service.

Planning for success is not the same as planning to avoid failure. Always ask, "Why will this fail?"

YOUR STRATEGY IS *NOT* AN EXECUTION PLAN (SO YOU NEED ONE)

Now you need to operationalize your SCIs. That requires *Execution Plans*.

An Execution Plan outlines the time-linked milestones and associated resource requirements (material, financial, and people) for each SCI. It identifies the *Executive Sponsor*—the Strategic Leadership Team member ultimately responsible for the SCI, the *Champion*—the person entrusted with managing its execution, *team members*, and periodic *contributors*. Finally, it documents the *ROS*—the expected return on strategy that justifies the SCI. Large companies often capture this using project management software. Mid-market companies, however, often develop their own template. Figure 8.1 provides a template for a Customer Experience SCI.

How do you make sure you're not burying your people, committing them to too many SCIs? The *Resource Matrix* is a helpful tool (see Figure 8.2). Matrix the names of your team against all your SCIs as well as the nonstrategic projects that fall outside their regular duties. Examine the totals. Are you setting people up to fail? Do you need to reallocate responsibilities?

BUILD RIGOR INTO YOUR PROGRESS TRACKING

How do you make sure your Execution Plans are being well managed? By conducting regular *Progress Tracking* meetings. Every month, the Strategic Leadership Team should meet to track and manage the progress of each SCI. For those meetings to be effective, here are five points to keep in mind:

1. Don't Get Mired in the Micro

It's easy for the conversation to get mired in detail—when meetings were held, who was there, what was said—yet lose sight of

OBJECTIVE: We must become a customer-centric organization

STR. CHANGE INITIATIVE: Redesign the in-store purchase experience

RETURN ON STRATEGY: Year 1: Increased customer traffic (+20%), revenue (+$2M), and "highly satisfied" ratings (28% to 50%)

FISCAL YEAR: _____ FY 2021

EXECUTIVE SPONSOR: Giselle

CHAMPION: Kai

TEAM MEMBERS: Rodney, Aaliyah, Pablo, Simone

MILESTONES:

	Description	Target Date	Status
Start		1/1	
1	Determine customer requirements and "wows" in a retail experience	1/31	
2	Measure the customer experience and identify service gaps	3/15	
3	Benchmark competitors	4/15	
4	Redesign the store layout and buying process	5/31	
5	Test in one location and get post-purchase feedback	7/15	
6	Revise and implement across the country	9/30	
7	Conduct assessment of Strategic Change Initiative	12/31	
Finish		12/31	

RESOURCE NEEDS: Customer research: $25k, Competitor research: $15k, Design and process consultants: $30k,

New furnishings and signage: $250k? TOTAL: Up to $320k

400–600 hours of internal resources' time

FIGURE 8.1 Strategic Management: Execution Plan

Employee Name	Strategic Change Initiatives						Department Projects						All
	Centralize purchasing	Segment customers	Implement ERP system	Open new branch	Launch "lite" product	Total Teams	Project #1	Project #2	Project #3	Project #4	Project #5	Total Teams	Grand Total
Ella	S		T			2						0	2
Rashon		C		S	T	3	C		T			2	5
Maria	C		S			2			T		C	2	4
Kirk		S		T	C	3	T			T		2	5
Soojin	T		C			2		T			T	2	4
Miguel	T		T			2		C	T			2	4
Kiana	T	T	T	T	S	5			T		T	2	7
Arjun			T			1				C		1	2
Daniel		T		C	T	3	T	T				2	5
Maryam			T			1						0	1
Amir			T			1			C			1	2
Laticia		T			T	2	T					1	3
Cassandra		T		T	T	3				T		1	4
Nicholas					T	1						0	1

LEGEND: S – Sponsor   C – Champion   T – Team Member

FIGURE 8.2 Strategic Management: Resource Matrix

the big picture. Yes, you should record and follow up on important action items, but the focus of each update should always be
the time-linked milestones. *Did we meet our time-linked milestones?*
Checking the boxes for individual action items doesn't matter if the
milestones aren't being met.

2. Make Sure to Measure; Measure to Make Sure

How do you define progress and success? Timely completion of
milestones is one way, but that reflects activity, not necessarily
results. The milestones were met, the SCI was implemented, but
did it make a difference?

To determine the impact of executing the SCI, develop a
Measurement Matrix, a tool that outlines metrics, targets, and
reporting requirements. Figure 8.3 outlines a Measurement Matrix
for the Customer Experience SCI. Let's say you decide that the
best measure of progress and success is "delighted customers,"
defined as the percentage of survey respondents over a one-month
period who rate their experience as "9" or "10" on a 10-point scale.
Your Commit Goal for the last month of the fiscal year is 50 percent. Your Aspire Goal is 60 percent. The quantitative milestones
(don't confuse these with your Execution Plan milestones) repre-
sent intermediate targets throughout the fiscal year. Results will be
depicted on a line graph with monthly data points showing actuals
versus milestones and goals.

Why develop a Measurement Matrix? According to one VP of
Finance, "It forces you to define, clearly and specifically, what you're
measuring, in what units, what is included, and what is excluded. It
removes any ambiguity in how people might interpret the metric
and what success looks like."

Strategic Initiative:	Redesign the in-store purchase experience
Champion:	Kai

METRICS	
Name	Delighted customers
Definition	% of customers who rate their experience 9 or 10
Units	1–10 scale (Strongly disagree to Strongly agree)
Measurement instrument	Post-purchase text survey
Measurement frequency	Offered to every shopper after every purchase
TARGETS	
Commit Goal	50% (currently 28%)
Aspire Goal	60%
Milestone #1—Jan	30%
Milestone #2—Feb	30%
Milestone #3—Mar	30%
Milestone #4—Apr	30%
Milestone #5—May	30%
Milestone #6—Jun	30%
Milestone #7—Jul	32%
Milestone #8—Aug	35%
Milestone #9—Sep	39%
Milestone #10—Oct	44%
Milestone #11—Nov	47%
Milestone #12—Dec	50%
REPORTING	
Format	Line graph showing the fiscal year, updated monthly
Elements	Commit Goal, Aspire Goal, Milestones, Actuals
Forum and frequency	Strategic Leadership Team meeting—monthly
Notes	Provide an incentive at the point of purchase (monthly prize-draw of $100) for each shopper to complete the 1-minute text survey

FIGURE 8.3   **Strategic Management: Measurement Matrix**

3. Don't Get Stuck in the Past

When reviewing measurable results, it's easy to focus on the past and neglect the future. Yet there isn't a lot of value in simply discussing what happened. The value ultimately lies in understanding why it happened, forecasting what is likely to happen, and then deciding what you intend to make happen.

The *Analysis-Action Ladder* is a helpful tool that reminds teams to be future-focused when discussing results and not to keep rehashing the past (see Figure 8.4).

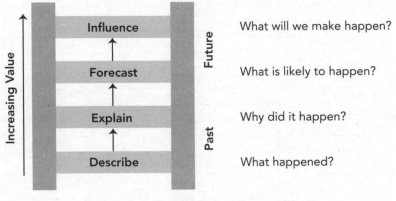

FIGURE 8.4   **The Analysis-Action Ladder™**

4. Don't Accept Weak Excuses

When commitments aren't met, it's tempting not to call out weak excuses. Why? It avoids confrontation. Yet by tolerating failure you become complicit in it.

Constructively challenge team members whenever a commitment isn't met. Be curious. Ask: "Can you explain why the commitment wasn't met?" "What could have you done differently to make sure it was?" "What will you do differently in the future?" Sure, there might be a valid reason. Often, there isn't. It's a lack of commitment. Despite all the excuses, rationales, and justifications, if something absolutely has to get done, then people almost always figure out a way to do it.

5. Celebrate Wins, Big and Small

It's easy to keep driving forward and not recognize everything that gets accomplished. Yet every milestone executed on time is a win. Celebrate. Help people feel good about their efforts and what they've achieved. It doesn't have to be a big production; it could be as small as simply saying "Great job!" and having a round of applause. Or it could be bringing in food to celebrate, recounting what was done, and recognizing those who played a role in it. Stay focused on the big picture, but make sure to recognize the small wins along the way.

THREE STRATEGY TRIGGERS

The Scottish poet Robert Burns inspired the saying, "The best laid plans of mice and men often go awry." A poet of the boxing ring, Mike Tyson, once said, "Everyone has a plan, until they get punched in the face."

You can't be dogmatic about your Strategic Framework. The world is ever-changing. Strategy has to be adaptive.

1. Reconstruct

The Strategic Management Process should have a regular cadence, typically, annual. That doesn't mean your Strategic Framework will change each year, but the entire framework should be *subject to change*. Each year, rigorously challenge and, as required, reconstruct your Strategic Framework. While your strategic thinking, and even your SCIs, might extend beyond a year, they should be assessed and validated no less than annually.

The most common trap when rethinking your Strategic Framework is to succumb to the *sunk cost fallacy*. This is when you continue down a questionable path because you've already invested a significant amount of time, money, and effort. The thought of all that "going to waste" leads you to soldier on in the hope that you'll recoup it. Reframe your thinking. Sunk costs are already sunk, not a justification for throwing good money after bad. Always reserve the right to do what makes sense, which sometimes means knowing when to stop.

2. Recalibrate

Much can change in a year. That's why it's helpful to recalibrate your Strategic Framework (once or twice depending on the pace of change in your industry). Schedule a full day with your Strategic Leadership Team to assess new information and data, attack your assumptions, discuss implications, and make needed revisions. Recalibrating the Strategic Framework keeps it real and relevant.

At the same time, recalibrate your Strategic Management Process by asking questions such as "How effective are our Progress Tracking meetings?" "How can we strengthen our Execution Plans?" "Do we have the right people and right resources for each SCI team?"

Recalibrating the Strategic Management Process makes strategy execution more effective and efficient.

3. React

While the fiscal calendar triggers when you should reconstruct and recalibrate your strategy, real-time events can dictate that you need to immediately modify your strategy. The coronavirus pandemic is a perfect and painful example of such a real-time event. Natural disasters, such as hurricanes and tornadoes, are more common examples.

Here's how we reacted back when a massive hurricane—Hurricane Katrina—was bearing down on New Orleans. Client company Point Eight Power, a provider of generator control and power distribution systems, realized its people, facilities, and operations—*its entire business*—were at risk. The strategy couldn't be clearer: Ensure survival and minimize the effects of the disaster.

We urgently developed a *disaster response plan*, and within 72 hours of landfall, implementation was underway. We established seven-day-a-week, early-morning conference calls with Point Eight Power's Strategic Leadership Team. Knowing that the effect on people would be massive, we developed a mantra and enlisted everyone in our efforts to achieve it: "*A handful of success stories will emerge in the aftermath of Hurricane Katrina. We will be one of them.*" We identified a set of four guiding principles: (1) people first, (2) communication is king, (3) manage morale, and (4) honor the heroic efforts.

In less than three weeks, the company had set up a disaster control center in Houston; located all its employees; initiated relief efforts; established extensive, multichannel communications with employees, customers, and suppliers; repaired facilities and equipment; organized temporary, on-site living; and resumed operations. As a result, almost every delivery commitment was met, while many other companies were still assessing if they even had a business. Point Eight Power's customers expressed amazement at the speed of its recovery. Three weeks after that, at an all-employees appreciation event, the recognition of their heroic efforts and what they had accomplished brought tears to the eyes of everyone.

Sometimes your strategy gets punched in the face. That's the trigger for real-time strategy.

Of course, it's not just a global pandemic or a natural disaster that can trigger real-time strategy. The defection of your largest customer, the chance to acquire a major competitor, the loss of a critical funding source—any significant opportunity or threat can and should trigger it.

Adaptability is the key to survivability. Your strategy has to be dynamic. Reconstruct. Recalibrate. React.

INSTITUTE; DON'T JUST IMPLEMENT

The goal isn't just to *develop* a plan. And it's not just to *implement* the plan. The goal is to *institute* a robust, repeatable process for assessing, developing, and implementing strategy.

Matt Lewis, CEO of Braidy Corporation, describes it this way:

> We've been at this for several years and because it's an ongoing process it's kept everyone on the Leadership Team engaged and aligned. They're more focused, more cohesive, and they take ownership for executing what we need to get done. The process supports accountability. Without it, it's hard to imagine we would have achieved the strong results we have over the past few years.

How do you sustain the process and make sure nothing falls through the cracks? Develop and manage a control document such as a *Master Calendar* (see the example in Figure 8.5). Matrix all the key strategic activities against the months of your fiscal year. Then review the Master Calendar each month at your Progress Tracking meeting, and look ahead to what needs to be done in the coming months. Doing this, nothing gets overlooked or forgotten. It ensures the Strategic Management Process becomes *the* overarching management process for your organization.

ACTIVITIES	Jan	Feb	Mar	Apr	May	Jun	Jul	Aug	Sep	Oct	Nov	Dec	NOTES
Strategic Management Process (SMP)													
Assign research projects/prework for the next SMP cycle							X						
Confirm/revise customer and market research process							X						
Conduct customer and market research								X					
Distribute reports and discuss with stakeholders							X		X				
Confirm/revise employee survey process							X						
Conduct employee survey process								X					
Distribute reports and discuss with stakeholders									X				
Conduct meetings to reconstruct the Strategic Framework									X	X			
Reconcile the Strategic Framework with the budget										X			
Prepare for the One Team Meeting											X		
Conduct the One Team Meeting	X												
Prepare for midyear Strategy Recalibration meeting				X									
Conduct Strategy Recalibration meeting					X								
Conduct Progress Tracking meetings	X	X	X	X	X	X	X	X	X	X	X	X	
Budgeting Process													
Provide tools for capex and operational budgeting							X						
Identify ownership's goals									X				
Assess competitive market opportunities and threats									X				
Assess internal offerings, performance, and capabilities									X				
Develop draft budget									X				
Gain feedback and integrate strategic requirements									X	X			
Finalize budget										X	X		
Prepare for midyear Budget Recalibration meeting				X									
Conduct Budget Recalibration meetings					X								
Conduct Budget Management meetings	X	X	X	X	X	X	X	X	X	X	X	X	

FIGURE 8.5 Strategic Management: Master Calendar

Approach strategy as a *managed process*, not a planning event. Be rigorous in developing your Strategic Framework—the why, what, and how of your strategy. Be equally rigorous in managing execution. And be prepared to modify your Strategic Framework— reconstruct, recalibrate, and react. Do all of this with ruthless consistency, and you will develop and sustain the right focus.

TAKEAWAYS

- Free up time for the strategic work. Have your team members clear their plates of non-value-added activities.

- Identify and remove potential mines by asking, "Why will this fail?"

- Translate your Strategic Framework into actionable Execution Plans and conduct structured, monthly Progress Tracking meetings.

- Keep your strategy current and relevant: reconstruct, recalibrate, and react.

- Don't just plan strategy. Institute a robust, repeatable process for assessing, developing, and implementing strategy—strategic management.

PART III

THE RIGHT ENVIRONMENT

Leadership is the creation of an environment in which others are able to self–actualize in the process of completing the job.

—John Mellecker

Y ou've developed the right focus. Now you need to create the right environment, one in which every touch-point is aligned with your intentions. An environment that *your people experience* as ruthlessly consistent.

Why the right environment before the right team? Because most leader have a team in place. And until you create the right environment, you won't know for certain whether you have the *right* team. Once you create it, you'll know. In the right environment, most team members will flourish. However, some may not be up to what is required. In that case, Part IV, "The Right Team," will help you build the right team.

Overwhelmingly, leaders will say that most SCIs fail because of people-related reasons, not technical reasons. It's a problem of not creating an environment in which team members are energized and enabled to perform

Ruthless Consistency®

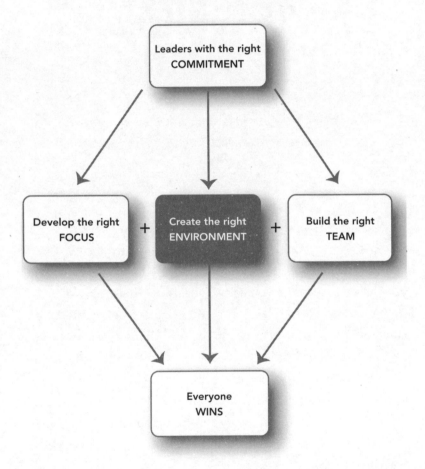

at their best. When you create an environment in which people are aligned, equipped, coached, supported, and valued, you create a culture of engagement, a culture of performance (see the Engagement-Performance Model on the next page).

How would you know if you've created the right environment? Let's check. Take three minutes and complete the following Alignment Questionnaire for leaders (you can also download it: RuthlessConsistency.com; password: MakeItHappen) . . .

Engagement-Performance Model™

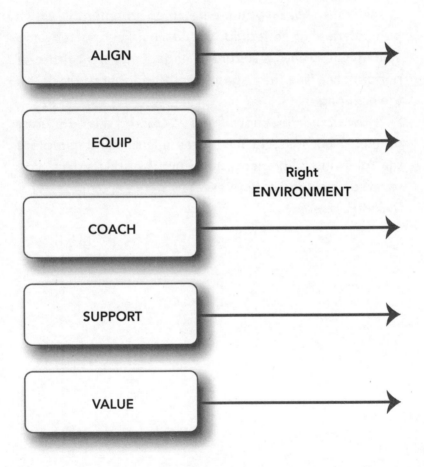

Alignment Questionnaire—Leaders

For each of the following items, check the box that most accurately represents the truth of the statement. If an item doesn't apply, then leave it blank. Total each of the columns at the bottom of the page.

STRATEGIC FOCUS	YES		NO
Our organization has a clear and concise definition of success	☐	*If NO, then stop*	☐

THE RIGHT ENVIRONMENT	YES	SOMEWHAT	NO
1. My team members understand and believe in the purpose of our organization.	☐	☐	☐
2. Team members understand our organization's goals.	☐	☐	☐
3. Team members understand what is expected of them in their jobs.	☐	☐	☐
4. Team members understand how what they do supports our purpose and goals.	☐	☐	☐
5. Team members are motivated to achieve what is expected.	☐	☐	☐
6. Team members have the skills to achieve what is expected.	☐	☐	☐
7. Team members have the information and knowledge to achieve what is expected.	☐	☐	☐
8. Team members have the resources to achieve what is expected.	☐	☐	☐
9. Team members have the time to achieve what is expected.	☐	☐	☐
10. Team members have the authority to achieve what is expected.	☐	☐	☐
11. I give team members meaningful feedback about their performance.	☐	☐	☐
12. I provide team members with guidance to help them improve.	☐	☐	☐
13. I reinforce team members for achieving what is expected.	☐	☐	☐
14. I hold team members accountable if they don't achieve what is expected.	☐	☐	☐
15. The right processes are in place to help team members achieve what is expected.	☐	☐	☐
16. Team members can influence how processes are changed or improved.	☐	☐	☐
17. Our policies support team members' efforts to achieve what is expected.	☐	☐	☐
18. We have the right positions on the org chart to achieve what is expected.	☐	☐	☐
19. Departments and locations effectively work together to achieve what is expected.	☐	☐	☐
20. Our facilities allow team members to achieve what is expected.	☐	☐	☐
21. Our equipment enables team members to achieve what is expected.	☐	☐	☐
22. I respect and trust my team members, and care about each one as a person.	☐	☐	☐
TOTALS:	☐	☐	☐

Done? How many "Yes" boxes did you check? What do you think is a good score? Here's a hint: Do you remember the title of the first chapter? What's more important than anything you do is *everything* you do. That means *any* critical factor misaligned could undermine everything. A good score is when you've checked every "Yes" box.

Most SCIs fail. You want to be one of the successful few? Create the right environment.

EVERYTHING STARTS
WITH HEADS AND HEARTS

My job as a leader is to make sure everyone in the company has great opportunities, and that they feel they're having a meaningful impact.

—Larry Page

IMPLEMENTING STRATEGIC CHANGE depends on people. You can have plans and goals and timelines and meetings, yet none of it matters unless you engage the hearts and minds of your people, and *align* them with what you want to achieve. It's not about *buy-in*; it's about *want-in*.

Engagement-Performance Model™

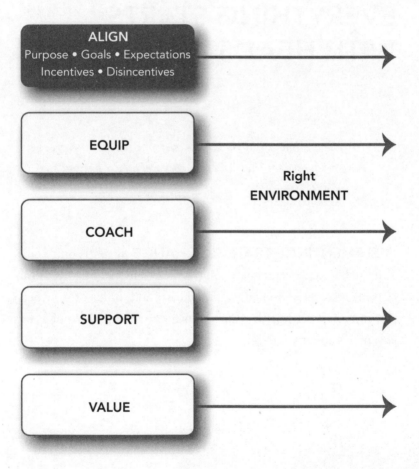

THE THREE TIMES YOU SHOULD ENGAGE YOUR TEAM

Most leaders think about engaging their employees once they've identified their SCIs. Too late. The decisions have been made. And the employees weren't involved in the process.

There are three times to engage your employees: *before*, *during*, and *after* you've developed your Strategic Framework. It starts with getting their *input*—their perspective on the issues, opportunities, and challenges facing your organization—before you make any strategic decisions. An anonymous, all-employee survey as well as focus groups with select employees are good first steps. (In either case, make the results available to your employees and let them know their opinions are a critical input to the Strategic Management Process.) Make sure to consider their ideas when developing your Strategic Framework.

Then, once a *draft* framework is developed, get their *feedback*. An effective way to do this is to conduct a half-day One Team Meeting involving *all* your employees. Seat them at round tables, present the draft Strategic Framework, and then have them discuss and flip-chart what they like about it, what concerns they have, and what questions they have. Have each table present their highlights to the entire team. Collect their outputs and review them later with the Strategic Leadership Team. Be open to modifying your Strategic Framework and, if you do, give the employees credit for it, acknowledging them for their ideas.

It's important that your team members have a voice—and know they have a voice—related to the direction of the organization. To be clear, "having a voice" doesn't mean "having a vote" or "getting to decide," or that all their ideas will be part of the final Strategic Framework. But when you ask for and consider their input, it sends a message of respect, that you value them and that their ideas count.

Once you've finalized your Strategic Framework, engage your employees again. Involve them, when appropriate, as members of your SCI teams. As for communications, you're just getting started.

CONNECT THE DOTS: PURPOSE, GOALS, AND EXPECTATIONS

For all that's been said and written about having a sense of purpose—as important as that is—what's even more important is that you *connect the dots* between purpose, goals, and each person's role—what is expected of them. What ignites purpose is when they clearly see how *what they do* as individuals contributes to the big picture, to success.

It had been a long day and now evening. Finishing off some client work, I packed up and walked out of our office at The Atlanta Consulting Group with Hyler, our CEO. As we exited the elevator and walked into the lobby of the building, off to the side a man was cleaning the floor. Hyler turned and approached him.

"Sir," he said, "I want to thank you for keeping our building so clean."

The man looked surprised, a touch suspicious.

Hyler continued, "Every day we have clients coming in and out of our office, and their first impression is this lobby. We want to project a professional image and have them feel comfortable. What you do makes a difference. I appreciate it."

The man cleaning the floor smiled. He stood a little straighter, his shoulders pulled back a bit. He felt validated. What he did mattered.

Yes, you want all your people to have a sense of purpose. Just make sure you connect the dots.

COMMUNICATE *WITH* PEOPLE, NOT AT THEM

Have you ever experienced this situation:

> You're meeting with your team because you want to keep them informed. After conveying what you need to convey, you ask, "Does anyone have any questions?"
> Silence.
> Check. Everyone's clear.

Don't bet on it. What you've just done is communicate *at* people, not with them. *Pushing* information at people doesn't make you an effective communicator. Yet too many leaders think of communications as a one-way stream of information.

Communicate *with* people. Imagine the same scenario, but instead of asking if anyone has any questions, you say something like this:

"Turn to the person next to you. Take two minutes. What's your number one reaction to what I've just said?"

The people in the group will naturally pair up and start to talk. They'll still be talking when the two minutes are up. Regain their attention and then ask for feedback from a random selection of team members:

"Terrell, what was a highlight of your conversation?" "Rebecca, what stood out for you?" "Mark, what was your partner's number one reaction?"

They'll openly share their feedback. Acknowledge their ideas and ask clarifying or follow-up questions as needed.

Communicate *with* people, not at them. When you give them a chance to discuss what you've said and provide feedback, and when you then acknowledge them, now you're truly engaging them.

THE PSYCHOLOGY OF CHANGE: OVERCOME THE DISINCENTIVES

Leaders often ask, "How do you make people want to change?" A better question is, "How do you overcome the reasons people *don't* want to change?"

The Number One Disincentive to Change

What do you think is the number one reason why people don't like change?

Fear. Fear of what? The unknown. "Will I be good at it or not?" "Will I like it or not?" "Will I be more secure or less secure in my job?" "Will I have more status or less status in the company?"

Uncertainty comes with change. It's entirely rational for people—even positive, ambitious, progress-loving people—to be fearful of the unknown. "What does this mean for me?"

How do you overcome that disincentive, the fear of the unknown? Make it known; communicate. *Overcommunicate* during times of change. You're familiar with what needs to be done. You've thought through the pros and cons, the risks and rewards. You're clear on what needs to happen, why, and how.

Your people aren't.

Talk about it once, and it gets forgotten. Talk about it a handful of times, and it might register. Talk about it continuously, and people start to realize it's important. That's why you need to overcommunicate during times of change. What needs to get accomplished, how it will get accomplished, and why it needs to get accomplished. Answering why is especially important. Because your people are thinking: "Why don't we just keep doing what we've been doing? "Why change?" "Why this change and not something else?" "Why now?" "Why here?" "Why me?"

Answering "why" provides context and meaning. People are far more likely to embrace the what and the how once they understand the why.

Here's how you might approach a conversation:

"Chen, you're probably thinking, why do we need to change? That's natural. Let me explain why we're changing . . ." *(Identifying with Chen lets her know you don't think she's being unreasonable. She becomes more receptive to your explanation.)*

"Here's what (our competitors are doing/our customers are telling us). If we don't change, here's how it's going to hurt us . . . If we do change, here's how it's going to help us. . ." *(Outlining the "why"—the consequences of changing or not changing—helps her understand the thinking behind the decision.)*

"Let me pause and get your reactions, and answer any questions you might have." *(Messaging that you're communicating with Chen, not at her.)*

"Let me give you a little more detail about the change we're undertaking (explain) and how we're planning to implement it (explain)." *(Reducing uncertainty and the resulting fear.)*

"Here's what you can expect, and here's how we're going to support you . . ." *(Messaging that her needs have been taken into account.)*

"Chen, I'm interested in your thoughts. What are we missing? How else can we help you and the team be successful as we go through this?" *(Involving Chen in the process and acknowledging that you may not have all the answers.)*

How do you think Chen is likely to respond to a conversation like that? Far better than if you didn't have the conversation.

Overcommunicate. If you think you're communicating often enough, then you're probably not. If you think you're overcommunicating, then you're probably communicating often enough.

> *Overcommunicate during times of change.*

Other Disincentives

Aside from fear, there are other disincentives to change. Many speak to a person's identity. For example, no one wants to look stupid, appear incapable, be embarrassed, or feel rejected by their peers. That's why it's important to create a safe environment for people. Let them know there will be a learning curve for everyone (they're not stupid), that everyone will struggle at first (they're not incapable), that everyone will make mistakes (they shouldn't feel embarrassed), and that everyone needs to support each other (they won't be rejected).

Before you implement any strategic change, think of why people might not want to change. Ask them about their concerns. Then take steps to overcome the disincentives.

THE PSYCHOLOGY OF CHANGE: TAP INTO THE INCENTIVES

Incentives. What comes to mind when you read that? Money? That's what comes to mind for most people. Don't just think money, and don't *first* think money. There is substantial research that suggests we overemphasize and over-rely on money as an incentive.[1]

Tap into the psychological incentives that lead people to change. Some of these incentives relate to their jobs. If the change makes their jobs easier, safer, faster, more interesting, or more enjoyable, then they're likely to support it. Some incentives relate to the work environment. If the change provides them with more autonomy, a sense of belonging, or a feeling of being supported, then they're likely to embrace it. Some incentives point to opportunity. If the change allows people to fulfill their desire for greater responsibility, challenge, or growth, then they're likely to pursue it. And some incentives speak to people's identity. If the change gives them a sense of purpose, of making a meaningful contribution, of being valued for those contributions, then they'll feel good about themselves, and change will feel natural.

When you tap into the psychological incentives that influence human behavior, you go a long way toward creating *want-in*, not just buy-in.

YOU *DON'T* NEED TO GET EVERYONE ON BOARD

One of the biggest misconceptions about strategic change is that you need to get everyone on board.

You don't.

Yes, you *want* to get everyone on board, but what you *need* is critical mass. Don't be held hostage by the *recalcitrant few*. The trap of thinking you need to get *everyone* on board is that you spend far too much time trying to convince, coerce, and cajole those least willing while neglecting those most receptive to change. And by focusing on those least willing, you unwittingly empower them because they can withhold what you want: their support.

Change the dynamic. Ignore the least willing (unless they're actively poisoning the environment, in which case you have to take prompt and decisive action). Focus first on the *promoters*, those at the front end of the curve who are excited about the change. Encourage them; support them; trumpet their successes. That creates "pull" and draws the *cautious many* in the middle of the curve. Now you're building critical mass. The people at the back end of the curve, the recalcitrant few, start to feel isolated, left out. As a result, some of them choose to join the movement. Welcome them with open arms. And there will always be a few who just don't want to get on board. Now you have a question to answer: Do they still belong in their current role, or even in your organization?

Invest your time and energy where it will generate the greatest return. Give everyone a chance to get on board. But don't be held hostage by those who won't.

REMEMBER THE SECOND PRINCIPLE: IT'S WHAT *YOUR PEOPLE* EXPERIENCE

You could engage your team before, during, and after you've developed your Strategic Framework. You could connect the dots between purpose, goals, and individual expectations. You could communicate *with* people, not at people. You could overcommunicate during times of change. You could remove the psychological disincentives to change and tap into the psychological incentives. You could focus first on those most eager for change. You could do all of that and *still* not engage the hearts and minds of your team members. Because what you do is not as important as what *they* experience.

Yes, do all those things, but be concerned with what *they* are thinking and feeling. Assume your communications *aren't* having the desired effect until *they* convince you otherwise. Ultimately, *their* hearts and minds are what drive their decisions and actions. And if you don't engage them—no, if *they* don't feel engaged—then you won't succeed.

TAKEAWAYS

- Engage your people before, during, and after you develop your Strategic Framework.

- Connect the dots between purpose, goals, and what you expect from each team member.

- Communicate *with* people, not at people.

- Remove the psychological disincentives to change; then tap into the psychological incentives.

- Give disproportionate attention to the promoters of change, not the recalcitrant few.

- Validate everything you do from the perspective of your people.

EQUIP THEM TO SUCCEED, NOT TO FAIL

Give us the tools, and we will finish the job.

—Winston Churchill

ARE YOU EQUIPPING YOUR PEOPLE to succeed or setting them up to fail? Don't align their hearts and minds with winning if you're not willing to provide them with the knowledge, skills, resources, and authority to make it happen.

Consider this: If I give you a sense of purpose but not the *resources* to fulfill it, how will you feel? Frustrated. If I provide you with skills but not the *authority* to apply them, what will you think? That I don't trust you. And if I give you authority without the *knowledge and skills* to use that authority wisely, what kind of decisions will you make? Bad ones.

Once you've got your team pointed in the right direction, now you have to equip them.

Engagement-Performance Model™

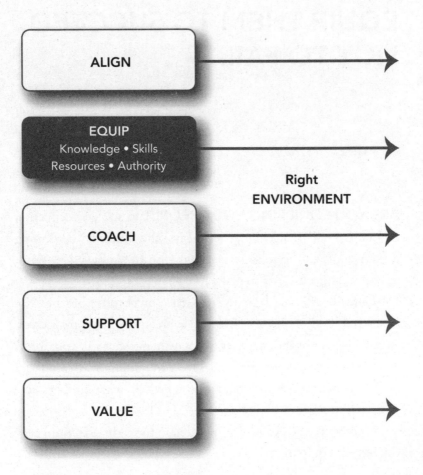

WITHOUT KNOW-WHAT AND KNOW-HOW, THERE'S NO WAY

Let's say your strategy is to provide an impeccable customer experience. Do your people know what that looks like? Do they know how to deliver it? Do you constantly discuss it? Do you role-model it? Do you embody it with ruthless consistency? Here's an example of what it looks like when you do:

> We arrived in Cusco, Peru, the historic capital of the Incan empire. Our intent was to explore the city for a few days before going on a five-day trek to Machu Picchu. We decided to stay at the Hotel Torre Dorada, a modestly priced boutique hotel with exceptional ratings and a reputation for extraordinary service. Of course, I was intrigued—would the service live up to the reputation?
>
> Our first touchpoint was Martin, the hotel's shuttle driver, who greeted us at the airport as if we were old friends. He was a fountain of helpful information, anticipating our various needs regarding meals, transport, and how to cope with the effects of altitude (Cusco is at an elevation of 11,200 feet). The goal of everyone in the hotel, he added, was that our total experience in Cusco would be fantastic.
>
> When we arrived at the hotel, Monika, the front desk attendant, greeted us by name. She was beaming, and happily went above-and-beyond to fulfill our requests. The following morning, we met the breakfast staff, who could only be described as joyful. Hmmm, was that the secret to the remarkably tasty omelets?
>
> On our final day I had a chance to speak with Peggy, the engaging and spirited proprietor. I asked how her staff was able to provide such consistently first-rate service. "Hard

work," she said with a wry smile. "We discuss it all the time. I ask my staff to imagine how it would feel if they were in another country, another culture. How would they want to be treated? What would make them feel comforted? Well taken care of? It's important that my staff know what our standards are and how to take care of our guests. And that I show them, so they know what to do."

Then she happened to look down at my coffee cup. "Oh no," she said, and immediately stepped aside to make a phone call. I looked down at the cup and noticed a tiny chip. Two minutes later a woman arrived, the head of housekeeping.

"This cup has a small chip in the rim," Peggy pointed out. "Could you please replace it? We can't have that for our guests."

The woman nodded, smiled, and went to replace the cup.

"As I was saying, hard work! Every detail has to be just right."

THE MAGIC OF MICRO-TRAINING

Do your people get the training they need to execute your SCIs? If not, why not? One likely reason is time. Developing people takes time, and how do you find the time when everyone is already maxed out?

Here's a solution we've found to be very effective: *Micro-training*. Twenty-minute, single-topic modules. One process, one concept, one model, or one practice. Yes, it's hard to get people away from the office, out of the plant, or off the road for a full day. But you can often pull them aside for 20 minutes.

There are three keys to an effective Micro-training module:

1. **Present the single topic.** Keep it simple; keep it focused. Use real-world examples whenever possible. Use support media—videos, images, charts, and checklists—to bring the topic to life. If the single topic is a behavioral skill, then explain it and role-model it.

2. **Have them process it.** Give people an opportunity to process what you've conveyed. Have them form groups of two or three and give them one or two questions to answer such as: "What do you like most about this concept?" "How could you apply this in your job?" Again, if the single topic is a behavioral skill, have them role-play it, not just talk about it. Bring everyone back together for a quick debrief. Draw conclusions, answer questions, and summarize the single topic.

3. **Give them a takeaway.** Give them a handout, weblink, resource, or something else they can refer to and that you can refer to with them. This helps to cement the Micro-training.

Micro-training has several advantages over conventional training. First, individual modules don't take a lot of time. As a result, there's minimal disruption to your day-to-day operations. Second, because the focus is limited to a single topic, people are more likely to retain and apply what they've learned. Third, when done regularly—every couple of weeks, for example—you can build a lot of know-what and know-how over time.

DON'T JUST TRAIN; DEVELOP

Don't just think "training"; think "development." Training is important, but training is just one of many ways to develop your people, and depending on the knowledge or skills required, it may not be the best way.

You can also develop people through coaching, mentoring, job shadowing, peer advisory groups, books, articles, videos, webinars, seminars, podcasts, vodcasts . . . there are more ways than ever to develop people. Don't simply default to training. Ask yourself, "What is the *most effective way* to impart the knowledge and develop the skills that each person needs?"

Keep in mind that you may want to develop more than just job-specific skills. Depending on the person's role, you may want to develop interpersonal skills, self-management skills, product knowledge, industry knowledge, or overall business knowledge. The question is, what knowledge and skills do your people need to perform at their best?

WHAT'S YOUR RETURN ON DEVELOPMENT?

Another reason why companies don't do more to develop their people is cost. While there is clearly a cost of developing people, you should also consider the cost of *not* developing people.

Whenever you discuss cost—better thought of as *investment* in the case of people development—you also need to consider the return. Ask, "What is the return we're getting on developing our people, and how would we know?"

You would know by systematically evaluating it. As a framework, I like Donald Kirkpatrick's *Four-Level Model of*

Evaluation: (1) reaction, (2) learning, (3) behavior, and (4) results.[1]

Imagine you've got a manager who does a poor job of providing performance-related feedback as evidenced by his employee survey ratings. Together you decide that, to improve, he'll spend a day shadowing another manager who rates highly in providing performance-related feedback. He also commits to watching an online video showing the steps and techniques of providing effective feedback.

After he's done both, you might get his *reaction* by asking what he thought about his shadowing day as well as the video. To determine what he *learned*, you might ask him to tell you or show you what he recalls. So far, so good, but until it's applied it's all just theory.

The next step is to observe the manager's *behavior* or ask employees if they've observed changes in the manager's behavior. Finally, as a measure of *results*, you could conduct a follow-up survey to see if the manager's ratings improve. Do his employees feel he now does a better job of providing performance-related feedback?

Progressing through the four levels of evaluation provides increasingly strong evidence for the effectiveness of developmental activities. While it takes time and effort to evaluate all four levels, you'll be far better equipped to answer the question, "What is the return we're getting on developing our people, and how would we know?"

DON'T DO MORE WITH LESS; DO LESS WITH MORE

"Do more with less." It's one of those mantras that we assume every leader should embrace. And why not? Doing more with less means

greater efficiency and productivity. Yet the unintended consequence of doing more with less is that we often under-resource SCIs, increasing the likelihood they will fail.

Which resource are you most likely to shortchange? When you ask employees, they'll often say, "time." They want to do a good job, they want to meet expectations, but they simply don't have the time. So what happens? They cut corners, things fall through the cracks, and doing the bare minimum becomes the standard. For many well-intended employees, the game is no longer about doing a first-rate job; it's about trying to keep all the plates spinning. That's frustrating for people who hold themselves to a high standard, who want to excel, and who are committed to success. They start to resent you because you're the author of their circumstance.

Of course, a shortage of time may be symptomatic of not having enough people. I've had to convince more than a few mid-market company CEOs that hiring an executive assistant was a worthwhile investment, that their time was better spent driving and supporting strategic change than sending out meeting invites and arranging travel plans. Finally, after hiring an executive assistant and then looking back, all of them said the same thing, "What was I thinking?!"

Don't do more with less; do less with more. That doesn't mean throwing resources at people or people at projects. It means concentrating *sufficient* people and resources on the critical few SCIs that absolutely must get implemented. If you're mounting an expedition to climb Mt. Everest, you'll need more than two people in T-shirts and flip-flops.

To be fair, it's not always easy to know how much is sufficient. Sometimes a lack of resources forces people to be *resourceful*. That was the case in the 1990s when NASA was planning the Pathfinder mission to conduct scientific experiments on the surface of Mars. As a result of severe budget constraints, a key objective was to complete the mission at *one-fifteenth* the (adjusted dollar) cost of previous Mars missions. This serious constraint spurred a number of innovations, the most famous being the use of airbags for the landing module. The idea was to "drop" the landing module to the planet's surface instead of relying exclusively on costly retro-rockets. Once it hit the planet's surface, the well-cushioned module would bounce up and down (over 15 times at a height of up to 50 feet, as it turned out) before coming to rest. At that point, the airbags would deflate and retract, allowing the exploratory vehicle to exit the landing module and begin the scientific part of the mission.

Yes, you should challenge your people to be resourceful and to innovate. But don't use that as an excuse to under-resource what must get done. Do less with more.

THE DARK SIDE OF EMPOWERMENT

"I don't like to micromanage," says the leader. "I like to give my people the freedom they need to make decisions and take action."

It's now well accepted that for your people to have a sense of fulfillment and to perform at their best, you need to empower them. Right?

There's more to it than that. Empowerment on its own is no panacea. It's just one element—yes, a very important one—in an environment designed for performance and results. But empowerment without direction leads to chaos. Empowerment without resources leads to frustration. Empowerment without knowledge leads to poor decisions. Empowerment without skills leads to well-intended failures. If all you do is empower your people, then you're setting them up to fail.

The dark side of empowerment is that it provides a ready-made excuse for managers who are lazy, who have fooled themselves into thinking that management no longer involves managing. Then, when things don't work out, they can simply blame their so-called empowered employees. If you say you're empowering your people yet do nothing to support them, then your people won't feel empowered; they'll feel *abandoned*. Set up to fail by a manager who lacks the understanding or discipline to know the difference.

LEVELS OF AUTHORITY

Many leaders mistakenly think of empowerment as all-or-none. "Our employees are empowered," they announce, as if it applies without limits in all situations. Is it any surprise then that employees believe they can make decisions and take action as they see fit? Once leaders belatedly realize and communicate there are limits, then those same employees feel betrayed and become cynical about their so-called empowerment.

You *don't* want your people empowered to make every decision in every situation or to take whatever action whenever. There are limits, and there should be. The question is, *what level of authority should your people have in which situations?* The authority to recommend? To decide? To act? And within what financial or operational limits? You might want a frontline manager to have discretionary spending authority of up to $500 but not $500,000. You might want a regional manager to provide recommendations about company policy but not to decide company policy.

There are also times for autocratic decision-making, when you and you alone should decide. I've seen leaders allow themselves to be held hostage by consensus—the idea that everyone has to agree. Well, if everyone has to agree, then anyone has the power to veto. Yes, you may want input from your team and even feedback on your preferred course of action, but there are times when your people simply want you to decide, and you should be the one to decide.

It's not about empowerment. It's about what level of authority people should have in which situations.

WHY PEOPLE DON'T WANT TO HAVE AUTHORITY

In general, people want the authority required to be successful in their jobs. They don't want to be powerless pawns. Yet don't assume that people *necessarily* want more authority. Have you ever encouraged people to make decisions and take action, but they won't? Why not? It could be that the *disincentives* associated with having authority outweigh the incentives. If they've been punished in the past for making mistakes, then why would they take initiative and risk getting punished again? The fear of retribution is a major reason why people don't want to use the authority they've been granted. Another reason is the fear of looking bad. Making a decision or taking action could result in a mistake. Others would judge them and might think they're incompetent or dumb. Safer to lie low and not be judged.

This was exactly the case at Talking Rain, a beverage company. Incoming CEO Chris Hall wanted to create a culture of urgency. To accomplish this, he needed to push decision-making authority down the org chart to those who best understood the relevant issues. Yet people resisted. Why? "Previously," said Hall, "bad decisions led to people getting embarrassed or even fired. Understandably, they wanted to protect themselves and push decision-making back up the ladder." Clearly, the environment was misaligned.

Hall took steps to realign the environment so that people would want to exercise authority and make decisions. He repeatedly communicated the importance of urgency and making quick decisions. He made sure that team members had access to the necessary data and analytics so they were equipped to make good decisions. To reinforce people who used the authority to make decisions, he sent them individual recognition notes. And most importantly, when people made decisions that didn't turn out well, the decisions and outcomes were positioned as learning opportunities, not reasons for punishment.

Make it *safe* for team members to make appropriate decisions and to take action. Equip them so they can make *well-informed* decisions and take *well-conceived* actions. Then, if they do make a mistake, reinforce them for taking initiative. Encourage them to learn and grow by asking two questions:

1. What have you learned?

2. What would you do differently next time?

Let your team know that mistakes provide improvement opportunities. Make the most of your mistakes.

AGAIN, THE SECOND PRINCIPLE: IT'S WHAT *YOUR PEOPLE* EXPERIENCE

You could train and develop the members of your team. You could provide them with the necessary resources. You could give them the authority to make decisions and take action. But you won't be successful unless *they* believe they're equipped with the knowledge, skills, resources, and authority to make it happen.

What you do is not as important as what *they* experience. Continually check in with them. Verify that their experience aligns with your intentions.

TAKEAWAYS

- Provide your people with the knowledge and skills they need to be successful. Consider Micro-training.

- Don't just think "training"; think "development." Ask, "What is the *most effective way* to impart the knowledge and develop the skills that are necessary?"

- Evaluate return on development using Kirkpatrick's Four-Level Model of Evaluation.

- Concentrate sufficient people and resources on the critical few SCIs that absolutely must get implemented.

- Don't use "empowerment" as an excuse for abandonment.

- Make it safe for people to use the authority you give them.

- Validate everything you do from the perspective of your people.

YOU'RE NOT A MANAGER; YOU'RE A COACH

You don't build a business. You build people, and then people build the business.

—Zig Ziglar

THERE'S A CRITICAL DISTINCTION between being a manager and being a coach. *Coaches take responsibility for the performance of their team and each team member.* Coaches view their role as helping team members perform at their best, helping them learn, improve, and grow.

Coaches are proactive; they take initiative. They're constantly experimenting, trying different approaches to see what works and what doesn't. "What buttons do I need to push?" "What levers do I need to pull?" "What do *I* need to do so my people can and will perform at their best?"

Rarely will the coach of a team sport talk to individual players about winning. Instead, the coach will talk about *performance* and *improvement*, focusing on what each player can control because if each player does what she can and should do, then the team result will take care of itself.

Engagement-Performance Model™

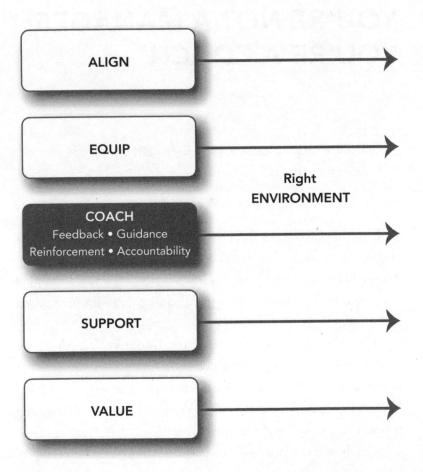

Two people are responsible for a team member's performance. You and the team member. You're responsible for creating an environment in which each team member can perform at their best. Each team member is responsible for performing. Both you and the team member play a critical role; both of you must be committed.

It's all too easy to blame the players when the team isn't performing well or isn't getting the desired results. Well, Coach, what did you do to create a different outcome? Did you simply point to the playing field, assume your players would perform, and then show up after the game to criticize their performance?

You can't be successful unless your team is successful. Connect the dots. Your role is to do everything you can to help *your people* be successful.

> Coaches take responsibility for the performance of their team and each team member.

THE GOLDEN RULE OF COACHING

You don't motivate people. You *create an environment* in which the right people will be motivated. And that doesn't mean the same environment for everyone. The *Golden Rule of Coaching* is that different approaches have different effects on different team members at different times. Some need you to reinforce their every step to let them know it's OK. Others want you to point them in the right direction and then get out of the way. The upshot is that you have to know your people and know where their hearts and heads are at different points in time. Great coaches are *adaptive*.

Few have done it better and for longer than hockey coach Scotty Bowman. As a National Hockey League (NHL) coach for 30 seasons (over a span of 35 years), Bowman won nine Stanley Cup championships with three different teams—the Montréal Canadiens, Pittsburgh Penguins, and Detroit Red Wings. He took a fourth team—the expansion St. Louis Blues—to an additional three Stanley Cup finals. *Sports Illustrated* named Bowman the greatest coach ever in North American professional sports, noting his unparalleled success with different generations of athletes.

Bowman had an extraordinary ability to adapt. Consider that in the late 1960s a coach's authority was sacrosanct, players were expected to be professional in their dress and grooming, and the average salary in the NHL was less than $18,000 per year. By the early 2000s, a coach's authority was arguable, dress and grooming standards had become a free-for-all, and the average salary was almost $3 million per year. Yet Bowman took his first team to a Stanley Cup final in 1968 and won his final Cup in 2002.

Great coaches are masters of psychology. They know their people and what makes them tick. They know when to encourage, when to challenge, when to pressure, and when to back off. They're constantly reading their team members, assessing morale, evaluating mindset, and testing and fine-tuning their approach, all to conjure the right psychological environment that results in optimal performance.

How intentional are you in adapting your approach to individual team members and to the situational context? One size does *not* fit all. Coaching demands that you see the world from *their* perspective, not just yours.

> *Different approaches have different effects on different team members at different times.*

FEEDBACK AND GUIDANCE: HUMAN INFORMATION MANAGEMENT

There's a common misconception about performance. It's that by repetitively doing something we automatically get better. That experience translates into improvement. Yet I'm reminded of what my doctoral supervisor, Ian Franks, used to say: "Practice *doesn't* make perfect. Practice makes *permanent.*"

Have you ever gone bowling? If every time you released the ball the lights went out, you couldn't hear what happened, and no score was shown, how much better would you get? You wouldn't. Because without any *feedback* you wouldn't be able to correlate your actions with the outcomes—associating what it *feels* like to throw the ball with what the ball *looks* like rolling down the lane, with what *happens* to the pins, with the *score* that results. Improvement depends on feedback. We don't learn simply by doing. We learn by *processing the feedback we receive* from doing. And not just any doing. The doing has to be focused and intentional.[1]

1. Don't "Review" Performance; Improve Performance

Many companies provide feedback through the annual performance review. How effective is that? According to an Adobe study of 1,500 office workers, almost two-thirds of employees and managers said reviews are an outdated way of managing performance. More than half of employees claimed that performance reviews have no impact on their performance and are a needless HR requirement. Of those surveyed, 22 percent said they had cried after a performance review (surprisingly, 25 percent of the men and 18 percent of the women).[2]

There's a better way. Take responsibility; be a coach. An overwhelming majority in the Adobe study (80 percent) said they wanted real-time feedback, not bundled feedback months later. That's why coaches provide SMART feedback and guidance—specific, meaningful, actionable, real time.[3]

Feedback *and* guidance? What's the difference? Feedback is about past performance; guidance is about future performance. Feedback is about what you did and what happened. Guidance is about what you need to do and what you intend will happen. If your goal is to *improve* performance, not just review it, then you need to provide both feedback and guidance.

Think of a manager monitoring calls in a customer call-center operation. By monitoring calls in real time, she can provide feedback and guidance before the call-center rep takes the next call: "The customer seemed irritated right from the start. It sounded like you immediately tried to find a solution but that didn't pacify him. What do you think would happen if you spent a little more time empathizing with the customer's feelings and even apologizing for our service failure before proposing a solution?"

2. Great Coaches Are "Performance Doctors"

Much like a medical doctor, a coach needs to *diagnose* the factors that are influencing performance and then *prescribe* what's needed to improve.

Remember the Analysis-Action Ladder in Chapter 8? The same questions apply when you adopt a coaching mindset. For example:

First: What happened?

"Sanjay, let's talk about the results from last month."

The purpose of this question is simply to identify recent outcomes.

Next: Why did it happen?

"Let's drill down. Why do you think you missed your target? Were those factors controllable, influenceable, or uncontrollable?"

The purpose here is to identify root causes and explain what led to the outcome. The answers may also point to what can be done to influence future results.

Then: What is likely to happen?

"If we continue doing what we've been doing, would we expect similar results in the future?"

This shifts the focus to the future and determines if it makes sense to keep doing the same things the same way.

Finally: What will we make happen?

"What do you need to do differently to produce a different outcome? How can I support you?"

This transitions the conversation from analysis to action with both you and the employee playing a role in creating a different outcome.

Diagnosis, prescription, joint responsibility. Both the team member and the coach play a critical role in performance improvement.

3. Great Coaches Ask Incisive Questions

You don't want a team of mindless order takers; you want a team that continually learns, grows, and improves. Strong coaches promote this by asking incisive questions. In the call-center example above, the manager didn't *tell* the employee to empathize and apologize. Instead, she packaged her opinion as a question by *asking* the employee what would likely happen if the employee were to empathize and apologize.

Here are some other examples:

When you disagree with an employee, help the person expand his thinking without making him wrong:

> "Can you help me understand why you think that?"
> "Are there other possible explanations?"
> "Would that still hold true if. . . ?"
> "What might be the arguments against that?"

When an employee is excited about an opportunity yet doesn't see the obstacles, help shift her thinking:

> "What could keep this from succeeding?"
> "How could we prevent that?"
> "How could we respond to it?"

When a well-intentioned employee makes a mistake, help the person benefit by asking:

> "What have you learned?"
> "What would you do differently next time?"

If you're always providing the answers, making the decisions, and telling people what to do, then don't be surprised when they don't learn, think, or take initiative. Why should they? You'll do it for them. Asking questions engages them in the improvement process—and you just might learn something as well.

> *We don't learn simply by doing. We learn by* processing the feedback we receive *from doing.*

REINFORCEMENT CEMENTS PERFORMANCE

While feedback and guidance provide the information that enables improvement, reinforcement and accountability provide the inspiration that drives it.

Ifyoudonttaketimetopauseandpunctuateyourteamsefforts withreinforcementrecognizingandcelebratingpeoplessuccesses thenyourteammemberswillfeeltheyreonaneverendingtreadmill andthatnothingisevergoodenougheventuallytheylllosemotivation andperformanceandresultswillsuffer

Did you get that? Let's try it this way:

If you don't take time to pause, and punctuate your team's efforts with reinforcement, recognizing and celebrating people's successes, then your team members will feel they're on a never-ending treadmill and that nothing is ever good enough. Eventually, they'll lose motivation, and performance and results will suffer.

Got it? Pause. Punctuate. Create moments that allow your team members to simply feel good about what they've accomplished. Then they'll be reenergized and ready to climb the next mountain.

1. How Should I Reinforce Them?

The first thing that likely comes to mind when you think of reinforcement and rewards is money. While money can be effective in some situations, there are far more effective ways to reinforce people than simply giving them money.

Over 60 years ago, Frederick Herzberg published his "two-factor theory" of human motivation, based on interviews with over 200 engineers and accountants. He said there are essentially two types of factors in the workplace: those that cause job satisfaction and are motivating, and those that cause dissatisfaction and are demotivating. Importantly, the two sets of factors are not the same. Achievement, recognition, and fulfilling work are prime examples of the first type. Company policies, supervision, and the work environment are prime examples of the second type.[4] Which means that while being recognized is highly satisfying, not being recognized is not highly dissatisfying. Company policies perceived as unfair can be extremely frustrating, yet policies perceived as fair don't cause people to jump for joy.

It's interesting to learn that compensation is an example of the second type. Meaning, that paying people well is not highly motivating. But paying them poorly can be highly demotivating.

The general finding about two types of factors—while subject to some criticisms—has been replicated in numerous studies and different contexts over the years. It's consistent with research conducted by the Gallup organization and outlined in the book *First, Break All the Rules: What the World's Greatest Managers Do Differently*. The authors identify 12 factors that determine high-performing individuals and organizations. Money is not one of them. Instead, people who feel their work is important to the purpose of the organization, who believe their opinions count, who are recognized for their efforts, and who feel their supervisor cares about them as a person are the ones who are engaged and who perform at a high level.[5] In a similar vein, in his book *Drive: The Surprising Truth About What Motivates Us*, Daniel Pink summarizes research and identifies three factors that, in the vast majority of circumstances, are key to workplace motivation and performance: autonomy, mastery, and purpose.[6]

Why? What is it about factors such as purpose, achievement, and recognition that resonate so powerfully with us? *Identity*. They speak to the core of who we are as individuals. When we have a sense of purpose, we have meaning. When we achieve, we feel successful. When we are recognized, we feel valued. These psychological reinforcers are powerful.

I clearly remember the most meaningful reinforcement I ever received at work. I was standing at the urinals in the men's room next to Hyler, our CEO at The Atlanta Consulting Group. Yes, really.

"Michael Canic," he said, "do you know what I like best about you?"

"Uhhh, no Hyler, I don't."

"When I ask you to do something," he continued, "I never have to think about it again."

And then he walked away. That was it.

Why was that so memorable? Because it spoke to my identity. That I was someone he could count on. Someone who was reliable. Someone he could trust. How did that make me feel? Valued. It made me feel good about who I am. And you can be sure it inspired me to be impeccable in living up to that belief—there was no way I was going to let anything slip through the cracks after that!

Fun can be another powerful motivator. Interjecting fun at work can be an effective way of reinforcing performance and results. The psychology of it is that you want your people smiling, laughing, and feeling good when they're around their colleagues and their managers. You want to build *positive associations* with the work environment.

Aside from connecting with the intrinsic motivators and aside from money, what else can a coach do to reinforce performance and results? *Symbolic gifts and experiences.* When you write someone a thank you card—no, not a thank you email, not a thank you text, but a thank you *card*—it says that you thought enough of the person to take the time and make the effort to write an actual card. That's symbolic. When you give your various team members something related to their personal interests—a gift card to their favorite restaurant, tickets to an event they've long wanted to attend—it says that you care enough to know who they are and what's important to them. Again, that's symbolic.

Just remember the Golden Rule of Coaching: Different approaches have different effects on different people at different times. Some people would be thrilled to be singled out for their accomplishments in front of their peers. Others would rather have pins stuck in their eyes. Some would relish the opportunity for more responsibility. Others would hate the pressure that comes with it. Some yearn for a promotion. Others dread being taken away from doing the work they love with the people they enjoy. For some, a simple and heartfelt "thank you" would mean the world. For others, a symbolic gift is something they would remember forever.

Reinforcement is multifaceted and has profound implications. There's much more to it than simply money. Don't get me wrong. As my dad used to say, "Rich or poor, it's nice to have money." Still, we default to money as a motivator far too often. Think about *the psychology of reinforcement.*

2. What Should I Reinforce Them For?

Big wins, small wins, completed SCIs, SCI milestones—reinforce your team for *legitimate* progress and success. But don't focus exclusively on results. There are times when it's also helpful to reinforce the right activities, those most likely to lead to results.

I witnessed the downside of results-only reinforcement while consulting with a company in the distribution industry. There were two mid-level managers who oversaw geographic territories. One manager hit his annual financial target and received his bonus. The other didn't. Yet with the first manager, the results occurred because of favorable market conditions. He had no coherent plan, and it wasn't clear what action he took to drive the results.

The second manager had a well-conceived plan and reliably took action, but market conditions worked against her, so she didn't hit her target or receive her bonus. Understandably, she was upset, feeling the plan was unfair.

This situation isn't unusual. The obvious question: Were they being reinforced for the right things?

We decided to take a different approach: *plan-action-results*. While at the end of the day we need to get results, we also need to do the right things to *maximize the likelihood* of getting results. Things like developing a solid *plan* and reliably taking *action*. We designed the new bonus program so that if a manager got the results, but had no documented plan or couldn't show he reliably took action, then he wouldn't receive the full bonus. On the other hand, if a manager developed a solid plan, executed as planned, but didn't get the results, she was still eligible to receive a partial bonus.[7]

What did this approach reinforce? Planning. Intentional action. Learning. And, yes, most importantly, results. It sent a message that we intended to achieve results by design, not by chance.

Here's another example: We worked with a company in the risk management industry that was implementing a new CRM system. The implementation was floundering, and the Strategic Leadership Team was frustrated: "How do we get our sales reps to consistently put timely information into the CRM? They just won't do it!"

Implementing a CRM system is a common SCI, and one that commonly fails to live up to expectations. Despite investing in a simple, effective, and proven system; despite explaining to the sales reps why it was needed, how easily it could be done, and *how it could help them*; and despite providing training and support, it just wasn't getting done. Why? Sales reps generally dislike administrative tasks because they seem like a waste of time, time that could be better spent selling. And in this case, the sales reps were being reinforced, earning commission, whether they entered information into the CRM system or not.

Can you see where this is headed?

We decided to change the commission structure to reinforce them for the *desired activity* as well as the desired results. We made timely CRM data entry a condition of earning commission. What happened? Obviously, the sales reps didn't like it and they complained. But because they were motivated—*very motivated*—to earn commissions, they did it. Then it became a habit. Then the complaining stopped.

Yes, results are critically important. But it's easy to lose sight of the *process*, the critical activities that lead to results. If you reinforce your people for developing well-structured plans and reliably taking action, then they're more likely to achieve *and continue to achieve* results.

3. When Should I Reinforce Them? How Frequently?

It's better to reinforce people sooner rather than later. Don't wait for the year-end party to celebrate. The closer in time the reinforcement is to the performance and results, the more impact it will have.

It's also better to have smaller but more frequent celebrations. You don't need to invest a lot of time or money. It can be as simple as getting team members together, describing what was accomplished, thanking them, leading a rousing round of applause, bringing in food and drink, and giving them time to bask in their success. Done. Everyone feels good. Everyone is re-energized.

Should you reinforce your team every time something positive is done or accomplished? No. In general, psychologists have found that *variable ratio reinforcement*—reinforcing people only some of the time and at an unpredictable (yet sufficient) frequency—is more effective than continuous reinforcement. Why? Predictability can lead to boredom. There's no element of anticipation or surprise So don't reinforce your team members every time they do something well. But reinforce them more often than you think you should.

THE ABSOLUTE NECESSITY OF CONSTRUCTIVE ACCOUNTABILITY

Buckle up; the ride's about to get bumpy.

Do you struggle with holding team members accountable? If yes, then you're not alone. Most leaders do. Why? There are obvious psychological disincentives. It's confrontation. It's uncomfortable. It's unpredictable. It can get emotional. It takes time and energy. "Why can't they just do what I tell them to do?!"

So what do you do instead? You rationalize to yourself. "Maybe if I give it more time, it will get better." Really? Like by magic? Why would it get better unless you intentionally did something to help it get better?

"But if I let him go, I'll never find someone to replace him." Never? That's a long time. Yes, it might take a while, but you'll find a replacement.

Lacking the courage to hold the employee accountable, yet recognizing you can't allow him to continue in his role, you get desperate. You put him in the *Incompetence Protection Program*. You give him a new role, a new location, hoping no one will notice. You're hallucinating. Once you've finally run out of excuses and summon the courage to let the person go, what do the other employees typically say? "It's about time." "What took you so long?" "Finally!" They knew all along. So what were they thinking about you all along? You're weak. You weren't committed.

Here is the number one, indisputable, irrefutable, incontrovertible reason why you *must* hold people accountable (drum roll):

It has nothing to do with the underperforming few. It's for everyone else. Everyone else who bought into the dream, who's driving to make it happen ... and who then sees that someone isn't getting the job done. They start to get irritated, and think, "Why aren't you doing anything about the person not getting the job done?" Then they question, "Why should I bust my back to make this happen when you don't care enough to deal with the person not getting the job done? Maybe I won't work so hard. Maybe I should kick back a bit."

Congratulations, you've now demotivated the many because you won't deal with the few. The number one reason you have to hold people accountable has nothing to do with those few people. It's so you don't send a message to everyone else that says, "I am not committed to winning." That's the message you're sending, because if you were committed, you wouldn't tolerate what you've been tolerating. Ask yourself this: If your people don't believe that you are committed to winning, how likely is it that they'll be committed? Right. They won't.

Are you feeling uncomfortable? Good. I want the discomfort of you *not* holding people accountable to be more intense than the discomfort of holding them accountable.

The number two reason for holding people accountable *is* because of the underperforming few. If you don't hold them accountable, then they'll think what they're doing is OK. Why should they change? It's rational for them to think that.

Enough. Let's reframe your thinking and equip you so you can feel more confident and comfortable holding people accountable.

1. Don't Think "Accountability"; Think "Constructive Accountability"

For many, "accountability" has negative connotations. Yet it doesn't have to be negative. The purpose of holding people accountable isn't to berate them, belittle them, or bully them. It's to help them improve so they can achieve, meet expectations, and feel successful. Your intentions should be positive.

Replace the term "accountability" with "constructive accountability." It captures the intention of why you should want to hold people accountable. Being "constructive" has positive connotations. Don't think "accountability." Think "constructive accountability."

2. Constructive Accountability and Compassion Are Not Mutually Exclusive

Some leaders don't like to hold people accountable because they don't want to be thought of as mean or cold-hearted. We've got some more reprogramming to do. *You can be a kind, caring, compassionate person and still hold people constructively accountable.* It's not *that* you do it; it's *how* you do it.

In Chapter 6, I referred to a company whose Cultural Commitments revolve around caring. How does this link to accountability? Former CFO/COO Michelle Gleeson explains, "Caring is consistent with accountability. We care enough to have the tough conversations with people, to be direct with them. We care enough to want them to improve and be successful. It doesn't serve them if we beat around the bush. There are times when you have to say, 'I want you to succeed and I believe you can, but if this doesn't improve it could cost you your job.'"

Yes, if you berate, belittle, and bully people, that would be mean and cold-hearted. Instead, imagine a conversation in which you hold a team member constructively accountable by responding to "failure" with *encouragement* and *belief* in the person's ability to do better.

I remember a National Football League game between Phoenix and Seattle that ended in an unsatisfying 6–6 tie. Surprisingly, each team's kicker missed what should have been an "automatic" game-winning field goal in overtime. After the game, when asked about his kicker's performance, Phoenix coach Bruce Arians responded bluntly, "Make it. This is professional; this ain't high school. You get paid to make it."

And what did Seattle coach Pete Carroll say about his kicker? "He's been making kicks for us for years. He's gonna hit a lot of winners as we go down the road. I love him, and he's our guy."

Well. Which coach would *you* rather play for?

When holding people constructively accountable, keep your *desired outcome* in mind. As a coach, you want your kicker to make *the next kick*.

> You can be a kind, caring, compassionate person and still hold people constructively accountable.

3. How to Hold Team Members Constructively Accountable

It helps to have a road map for the constructive accountability conversation. The next time you have that conversation, follow this five-step process:

1. Convey the Common Purpose

Set the tone by identifying a common purpose. Let the team member know you're on the same team; you're allies, not adversaries. Show how the person's success is aligned with the organization's success:

> "Tori, I know you're committed to achieving the goals for your branch. That will help us reach our company goals. We'll make money; you'll get your bonus; everyone wins."

2. Confront Reality

Be prepared. Gather any data or information you need *before* the meeting. Discuss the situation with the employee calmly and directly. Focus on measurable performance or observable conduct, not abstract concepts like attitude. Make it a collegial discussion. The goal is to understand the current situation and the factors that are contributing to it:

> "Tori, your location has missed its goal by 10 percent each of the past three months. Let's talk about what's happening and why, so we can develop a solid understanding of the situation."

3. Take Responsibility

This is counterintuitive, but it's the key to a successful conversation. Ask the employee what *you* can do to provide support. It puts the person at ease and changes the dynamic of the conversation. It opens the door to having a real conversation about performance:

> "I'm here to support you. What do you need from me? How can I help you succeed?"

Of course, some employees will use this as an opening to roll out a list of excuses, all the things they supposedly need to be successful. That's OK. You get to decide, and you don't have to agree:

> "Tori, I'm not convinced we need to make that investment. The other branches are able to hit their numbers without it."

On the other hand, maybe the person identifies a legitimate need:

> "You're saying if we provide your team members with process improvement training, then you can work with them to capture the efficiencies we need. I like it. Let's make it happen."

4. Discuss Solutions; Provide Clear Expectations

Have the team member lead the discussion regarding what steps she can take to drive improvement. Then provide specific and reasonable expectations of what you expect by when:

> "Tori, given what we've talked about, I expect your location to be back on plan within 90 days."

5. Rigorously Follow Up

Before you end the conversation, lock in your next "check-in" meeting. This lets the person know that change is mandatory, not optional. Do this at each subsequent meeting until the issue is resolved.

Encourage the person. Let her know you believe in her. Thank her for her commitment:

> "Let's block in our next meeting—no more than 15 minutes—so we can monitor how things are progressing. How does two weeks from today at 10 a.m. look?
> "Tori, I believe in you, I know you can get things back on track. Thanks for your commitment."

What happens when you follow this process? Usually, one of two things: Either the results get back on track, in which case everyone is happy, or they don't, which means you have to re-emphasize your expectations in the check-in meetings. If the issue is serious enough, and still doesn't improve to an acceptable level, then you may have to let the person go. But don't be surprised if she comes to you first, saying she's had enough. Often, the disincentive of an employee having to regularly meet with you and explain why she's not meeting expectations becomes so great that she surrenders.

Your role then is to help her transition out of the organization with dignity. And you'll have a clear conscience knowing you supported her and gave her a fair chance to succeed.

Even by following this process the constructive accountability conversation will still feel somewhat uncomfortable. But that's the price of leadership: being comfortable with being uncomfortable.

Finally, recognize that your team members will often live up or live down to your expectations. That's why, even if you have doubts, you should convey 100 percent belief in their ability until they give you overwhelming reason not to (at which point, you need to take decisive action). Convey that you believe in them, and they just may surprise you. On the other hand, if you express a lack of confidence in their ability, they might stop trying, thinking that nothing they can do would make a difference.

4. Performance and Conduct Are Distinct . . . and Both Count

There are two things you should expect from your team members: *performance* and *conduct*. Performance refers to how well they fulfill the requirements of their job. Conduct refers to their behavior and how they interact with others.

The moment of truth comes when a top performer exhibits poor conduct. What do you do when your top salesperson berates and threatens a customer support rep? If you look the other way—after all, you might think, the person *is* a top performer—you send a strong message about what *you* value and what *you're* willing to tolerate. If the salesperson's conduct makes a mockery of your company values, then you've killed your credibility and allowed him to poison the culture.

Deal with performance and conduct as the two separate items they are. They don't average out. Great performance shouldn't excuse poor conduct any more than great conduct should excuse poor performance. Establish and communicate minimum standards for each.

> Great performance shouldn't excuse poor conduct any more than great conduct should excuse poor performance.

Oh, and what happens when you finally decide that high-performing yet much-loathed team member has to go? Everyone cheers. Morale improves.

5. Constructive Accountability Starts With You

Look in the mirror, Coach. It starts with you. Before you hold *them* constructively accountable, ask yourself, "Have I done what I need to do to give my team members a fair chance to succeed?" If not, then get to work. Constructive accountability starts with you.

DON'T FORGET THE SECOND PRINCIPLE

You could think like a coach and adapt your approach for each team member. You could diagnose performance issues, ask incisive questions, and provide SMART feedback and guidance. You could reinforce them to connect with their identity. You could hold them constructively accountable for performance and conduct. Yet it won't be effective if it doesn't match what *they* experience.

To perform at their best, *they* need to believe they're receiving helpful feedback and guidance, they're being reinforced for performance and results, and they're being held constructively accountable.

What you do is not as important as what *they* experience. Continually seek their feedback. Does their experience match your intentions?

TAKEAWAYS

- Take responsibility for the performance of your team. Deeply understand each team member's strengths, limitations, motives, and traits.

- Apply the Golden Rule of Coaching: Different approaches have different effects on different team members at different times.

- Be a performance "doctor" who asks incisive questions.

- Help team members improve by providing SMART feedback and guidance.

- Reinforce performance and results by focusing first on each team member's sense of identity.

- Hold team members constructively accountable for both performance and conduct.

- Start by holding yourself constructively accountable. Create an environment that gives each team member a fair chance to succeed.

- Validate everything you do from the perspective of your people.

HEROIC PROCESSES, POSITIVE POLICIES, AND THE SPACE BETWEEN THE BOXES

For every minute spent in organizing, an hour is earned.
—Benjamin Franklin

A LARGE, INDEPENDENT BOOKSTORE was suffering. Not only were sales being siphoned away by online retailers, but customer satisfaction was slipping. Finding books in the store could be confusing, availability was hit or miss, lines were often long, and overwhelmed staff would at times show their frustration. All things considered, the bookstore's future did not look promising.

When they asked us to help, our first and most obvious concern was that they weren't yet offering online sales. Yet we wanted to know if there was more to the story. Our assessment uncovered 19 root causes underlying customer dissatisfaction. Most were related to organizational design—processes, policies, and structure:

Engagement-Performance Model™

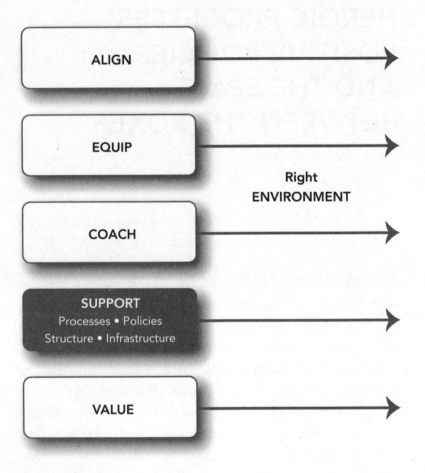

The configuration of the store was confusing and uninviting.

The organization of book subjects wasn't intuitive.

Signage was poorly located.

The book-ordering process was cumbersome.

The return policy was overly restrictive.

Staffing was inadequate.

The hours of operations were limited.

At the same time, we determined that the staff very much wanted to provide great customer service and understood its importance. Their frustration bubbled up from how "the system" was keeping them from providing great service. The problem here wasn't one of purpose, incentives, training, or coaching. The problem was the bookstore wasn't *designed* to provide a great customer experience.

Once we addressed the root causes by redesigning processes and policies, and changing elements of the structure and infrastructure, then the customer service metrics—as determined by post-purchase surveys—improved dramatically. The survey findings: 78 percent of respondents said it was faster and easier to locate books, 76 percent noted greater availability, 90 percent spent less time waiting in cashiers' lines, and 94 percent found the service attitude of the staff had improved. While, like many independent booksellers, this bookstore would only survive by offering online sales, improving the in-person customer experience was essential to maintaining the store's viability.

HEROIC EFFORTS AREN'T SCALABLE; HEROIC PROCESSES ARE

All of us have been on the receiving end of a service employee making a "heroic effort" to meet our expectations. We are deeply grateful, the employee feels a sense of satisfaction knowing she made a difference, and her company may recognize her as a role model for all employees.

It's a trap. Heroic efforts aren't sustainable and aren't scalable. What happens if the team member gets burned out? What happens if she leaves and isn't replaced by someone who makes similarly heroic efforts? What happens as your company grows, and heroic efforts are increasingly needed to make up for faulty processes? And what is the time and cost incurred from making heroic efforts?

Better to invest in "heroic processes"—processes that are sustainable and scalable, that survive individual employees coming and going, that can accommodate growth, and that are time and cost efficient.

We once worked with a trucking company that would go to extreme lengths to meet its delivery commitments. Managers vigorously encouraged employees to do whatever it took to get the packages delivered on time. Yes, they put the customer first and, yes, deliveries were largely made on time. Yet the consequences were that, overtime, contract labor costs, and employee turnover were all out of control, and vehicle accidents were far too frequent.

The new VP of operations realized the company needed to stop the insanity. He decided to form a team to redesign the package sorting and loading process. Identifying and fixing numerous inefficiencies, the company was able to significantly reduce the cycle time of package processing, allowing trucks to leave the warehouse earlier. As a result, overtime, contract labor costs, employee turn-over, and vehicle accidents all declined. The need for heroic efforts was replaced with a heroic process.

Is there ever a need for heroic efforts? Yes, but they should be the exception; heroic processes should be the rule.

Where should you start? Which processes should you make heroic? Start with the processes relevant to your SCIs.

Envision yourself in this situation:

You're out at a well-regarded restaurant for dinner. The server has taken your drink order, and you're now scanning the menu. Nothing jumps out at you. Best to see if there are any specials.

After a delay that's longer than it should be, the server returns with your drink, and asks, "Have you made any decisions?"

"Do you have any specials this evening? And what's your soup of the day?"

"Hmmm, I'm not sure. Let me go check."

Let me go check? You don't know?

After another delay, the server returns and says, "No specials this evening, sir. Just our regular menu. And the soup of the day is the minestrone."

"OK, I'll have the pan-fried trout. And a spinach salad to start."

"Very good. Thank you."

A few minutes later the server reappears. "I'm sorry, sir," he says. "It turns out that we don't have the trout this evening."

"No trout? Then I'll need to see the menu again."

"OK, I'll go get one."

What just happened? The server didn't know if there were any specials, didn't know the soup of the day, and didn't know that the trout wasn't available. And he didn't anticipate that you just might need to see the menu again! You've now been at the restaurant for over 15 minutes, the server has been back and forth several times, and you still haven't ordered. You're understandably irritated.

Now imagine you're the manager of that restaurant, and your SCI is to provide an outstanding dining experience. You should want to assess *every* process and *every* touchpoint that influences that experience, including the reservation process; the arrival, greeting, and seating process; the server introduction and ordering process; the meal presentation and dining process; the check delivery and payment process; and, finally, the departure process. If your goal is to provide an outstanding dining experience, then every detail, no matter how small, should be scrutinized.

Here's an example of a small but relevant process detail: At the end of your meal, the server may approach your table and say something like, "How was everything this evening?" If you're like most people, you'll reflexively answer, "Fine" or "Good." Which means that information is useless. The restaurant just squandered an opportunity to get valuable feedback that could help it enhance your experience.

Instead, imagine the server says, "Thank you for dining with us this evening, sir. If there was one thing we could do to make your experience even better next time, what would that be?"

You pause, taken aback by the question but, nonetheless, appreciative.

"I would have liked the scallops to be warmer."

"Very good, sir. We'll note that."

Asking that question prevents a reflexive answer and prompts the customer to think of one thing that you could improve. This "One Thing Better" approach was one of our recommendations to a restaurant owner whose goal was to consistently provide an outstanding dining experience. The servers would then record the "one-things," and the managers would chart their frequencies and, most importantly, take action to improve the most frequently mentioned one-things.

ARE YOUR POLICIES POSITIVE OR PUNITIVE?

As surprising as it might seem, yes, a simple policy could undermine your SCI.

One of our clients, a manufacturer of high-tech parts, decided to compete on speed. The company believed it would gain a competitive advantage if it were quick to respond, quick to quote, quick to manufacture, quick to deliver, and quick to repair. That was communicated to every employee.

There was just one problem. The company's expense reimbursement policy said it could take up to six weeks for employees to get reimbursed for out-of-pocket expenses. What do you think that did for the culture of speed? Exactly. It poisoned it. People became cynical. "Speed? Ya, right. Nobody seems too concerned about speed when it comes to my money. How about a little more speed in the accounting department?"

Contrast that with the policy at Signet Health Corporation, a healthcare management company with employees working across 18 states. Signet Health reimburses hospital-based employee expenses *the next day*. As Signet Health's president, Jerry Browder, explained: "It's one of the few, regular touchpoints we have with our remote employees. It's important they know we're there for them. And when new employees send in their travel and marketing expenses for the first time, they're always surprised to learn they will be reimbursed by direct-deposit the very next day."

Consistency. Signet Health's objective is that field-based employees feel well supported. Its policy is consistent with that objective.

MANAGE THE SPACE
BETWEEN THE BOXES

When you think of organizational structure, you probably think of the org chart—the pyramid of boxes and arrows, what reports to what, and who reports to whom. Inevitably, it results in silos—"us-versus-them." Whenever you have an SCI that involves more than one box on the org chart, ask yourself, "How should we manage the space between the boxes?" Here are five ways to do that:

1. "Parachute" Team Members into "Foreign Territory"

It's easy to make assumptions, typically negative, about *them*—the other departments, functions, or locations. A classic example involves sales and manufacturing. The sales rep thinks the manufacturing people are lazy because they "never" get the product delivered on time. The manufacturing supervisor thinks the sales reps are liars because they keep making promises to customers that manufacturing can't fulfill.

The best way to break down assumptions is to have people walk in each other's shoes and see through each other's eyes. "Parachuting" a team member into another department (or location) for a day builds a deeper understanding of what goes on in that department and the challenges that people face. Just as important, it builds rapport, and it humanizes "them." People spending a day together always find common points of interest.

Even more important is to leverage the experience by having the person who parachuted give a five-minute "Here's what I learned" presentation to the rest of her team. Then capture quotes for the company newsletter. Here is what one field employee in the restoration industry had to say after parachuting:

> I learned how important the Project Coordinator role is. Their work isn't given enough credit; the field has no idea how important they are. Omar's team really have their act together, and Jasmine is amazing at her job. Being a Project Manager isn't as glamorous as field techs think, either. There is a lot of work behind the scenes; it's not just schmoozing and golfing. And you have to be really good at time management to succeed.

Parachuting people across the spaces between the boxes goes a long way to breaking down "us-versus-them."

2. Establish a Representative Team

It's surprising how often SCI teams are made up exclusively of those *designing* the change without representation from those *affected* by the change. Always allow those affected to have a representative at the table. Not only do they need to feel heard, but they often have insights that can aid in the success of the SCI and help avoid what could cause it to fail.

Another situation that can benefit from a representative team is when an SCI touches more than one department, function, or location. An SCI to reduce customer complaints, for example, might have representatives from sales, operations, customer service, and technical support.

3. Create an Integrator Position

Sometimes it's helpful to create a high-level "integrator" position, someone tasked with ensuring consistency across the spaces between the boxes. For example, a VP of the customer experience can help to ensure that customers receive a similar standard of service regardless of the department they're dealing with. Such a standard might include setting a maximum call-wait time, providing a first name when engaging the customer, or making time-specific, follow-up commitments.

4. Handcuff People Together

If different functions need to collaborate to produce a desired outcome, then make it in their common interest to do so. Handcuff the functional heads together by tying part of their financial incentive to what they collectively achieve. If your SCI is to reduce the cycle time for construction projects, then a common incentive can drive collaboration and coordination between trades when it wouldn't otherwise occur.

5. Spotlight the Space Between the Boxes

Make managing "the space between the boxes" a standing agenda item in your Strategic Leadership Team meetings. Identify gaps and friction points, and discuss ways to overcome them. Anticipate potential gaps and friction points, and discuss ways to prevent them. In either case, commit to specific, time-linked actions.

IMPLEMENT WINNING INFRASTRUCTURE

Are your facilities large enough and configured in a way that enable you to achieve your objectives? Can your equipment reliably produce a quality product at the speed required? Is your equipment durable enough to produce the volume required without excessive maintenance? Do your IT systems provide you with the capability to capture, analyze, and interpret the information needed to successfully execute your SCIs?

Facilities, equipment, systems—the right infrastructure is essential, just as the right processes, policies, and structure are, to successfully execute your SCIs.

IT'S NOT ABOUT WHAT YOU DO;
IT'S ABOUT . . .

Institute heroic processes. Put positive policies in place. Establish the right structure and manage the space between the boxes. Ensure you have the necessary infrastructure. Do all of it . . . and you could still fail. Because to be successful, *your people* have to believe that the processes, policies, structure, and infrastructure enable them to be successful.

What you do is not as important as what *they* experience. Is their experience aligned with your intentions?

TAKEAWAYS

- Heroic efforts can be a trap—they're not sustainable or scalable. Better to develop heroic processes.

- Beware of policies that send mixed messages. Revise or eliminate them.

- Proactively manage the space between the boxes on your org chart.

- Ensure your facilities, equipment, and systems meet the requirements of your SCIs.

- Validate everything you do from the perspective of your people.

THE VALUE OF FEELING VALUED

*Imagine that every single person you meet has a sign
around his or her neck that says, "Make me feel important."*

—Mary Kay Ash

MY WIFE AND I ENJOY international travel. We love the feelings associated with adventure, with exploring. It's the emotional mix of anticipation, exhilaration, and apprehension. It makes us feel fully alive.

Wherever we go, I like to ask people about their work. I'll ask questions such as: Do you enjoy your job? Is it a good company to work for? Do you like your boss? Why? Why not? I want to understand their world, their context.

We were in the Wadi Rum desert in southern Jordan. With mountains jutting out from the desert sands like volcanic islands from the sea, it's a vast and staggeringly beautiful landscape, one that T. E. Lawrence (Lawrence of Arabia) wrote so passionately about.

We had traveled all-day by camel to arrive at our camp. After a restful night we were eager to explore. Zidane, our

Engagement-Performance Model™

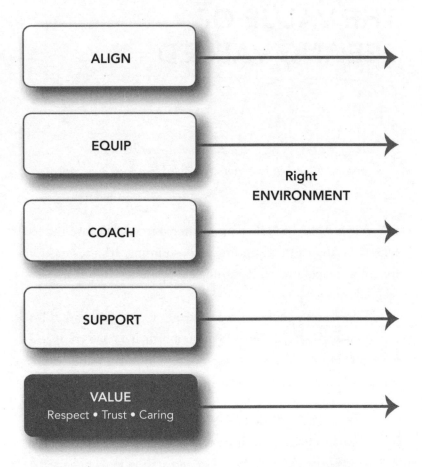

Bedouin guide, was leading our scramble up a desert mountain. After climbing a testy rock wall, we rested, and I asked Zidane about his work with the tour company. "I very much like being in the desert with the tourists," he said. Then, reflecting, he added, "I thought about starting my own business but I like the people I work with here."

And his boss, the owner of the company? "Attayak is a good and kind boss. He treats his people with respect. He trusts them. And if mistakes are made, by guides or tourists, he is straight with them. I respect him, and I like working for him."

In traveling to almost 50 countries, I have found that regardless of country or culture, race or religion, nationality or ethnicity, there are three universals that are core to a person's work experience: *respect*, *trust*, and *caring*. When people feel that you respect them, you trust them, and you care about them as individuals, then you connect with them at a human level—and they're likely to reciprocate those feelings.

It seems obvious. Yet how often have you witnessed the opposite, when people feel their managers *don't* respect them, *don't* trust them, and *don't* care about them as individuals? It undermines morale and performance.

When you fundamentally value people as people, it speaks to their identity. What does that have to do with implementing SCIs? People who feel valued are more likely to identify with your goals, to adopt them as their goals, and to work to achieve them. That's not *why* you should value people, but it's an *outcome* of valuing people.

DEMONSTRATING *RESPECT* SAYS MORE ABOUT YOU THAN ABOUT THEM

I had just delivered a daylong leadership workshop to the members of a trade association. Returning to the airport, I had some extra time and decided to get my shoes shined.

Franklin, the affable shoeshine guy, quickly engaged me in a conversation, asking me about my day and what I had done. I told him.

He immediately asserted: "Let me tell you something about leadership, my friend. I manage four people. Soon, I'll be opening another location here at the airport. And I will tell you that the most important thing about leadership—it doesn't matter what business you are in—is respect. Always be respectful of your people."

Well. Exactly right. Maybe I should have attended *his* workshop!

Demonstrating respect—consistently—speaks to what *you* fundamentally believe about people and how they should be treated. It sends a message that reinforces their sense of self-worth. The result is that people who feel respected are engaged.

When you *start* by respecting people—not because of their actions, not because they've "earned" it—it says more about you than it does about them.

DO YOU *TRUST* THEM EVEN IF THEY'RE NOT AS PERFECT AS YOU?

I was lucky. Early in my career I worked with a pioneering firm in the field of trust-based leadership, The Atlanta Consulting Group. Our gateway offering was a workshop called "Trust and Teamwork," which introduced leaders to the principles and practices required to build them. Those lessons have withstood the test of time.

A 2019 study of over 19,000 employees in 19 countries concluded that engaging people and having them perform at their best comes down to two things: teams and trust in team leaders.[1] Specifically, it's when people feel they're a part of a team—a group of people working collaboratively to produce a clear and desirable outcome—and have a trusted leader who helps them play to their strengths and recognizes them when they do. How much of a difference does it make? People are *12 times* more likely to be fully engaged when they trust their team leaders!

Trust is a two-way street. When you trust people, they're more likely to trust you. So why is it that leaders are reluctant to trust their people? Fear. The fear that their people might make a poor decision or do the wrong thing. Ah, if only they were as perfect as we are! Shouldn't leaders instead be fearful that they haven't done enough to prepare their people to make good decisions and take effective action?

If all the managers you've had never trusted you out of fear that you might do something wrong, how would that have made you feel? How would that have limited your learning? Your achievements? Isn't it better to prepare people, trust them, and then, if they do make mistakes, help them learn and grow?

DO YOU *CARE* ABOUT THEM AS PEOPLE? HOW WOULD THEY KNOW?

As a manager, it took me some time to learn that while you hire employees, human beings show up to work. They don't simply leave "the personal stuff" at home. They bring to work their ambitions and anxieties, hopes and fears, securities and insecurities, who they are and what they're dealing with. If you're oblivious to all that, you're likely to push the wrong buttons at the wrong times and disengage your people.

> *You hire employees, but human beings show up to work.*

If you ask how their fishing trip went, how their daughter is doing at university, how they like their new car, how their elderly mother is doing, then you're sending a message that you care. You care enough to know what's important to them and to want to know what's important to them.

If you send a gift basket of appreciation home to their partner when they've been traveling a lot, or give them a day off to be with their sick child, or bring in a masseuse to give massages during a stressful period at the office, then you're sending a message that you care. You care enough to identify with what they're going through.

I've heard some leaders say there's no place in business for feelings, that people should be rational, not emotional. Here's the irony: When you treat people as people first, employees second, they become better employees. Managing the emotional *is* rational.

IT'S NOT ABOUT WHAT *YOU* DO, IT'S ABOUT . . .

Demonstrate respect. Trust them. Show them you care. And as you know by now, what *you* do is not as important as . . . (complete this sentence).

Got it?

- When you treat people with respect, they feel confident. Confident people are more willing to stretch themselves in pursuit of goals.

- When you trust people, they feel a sense of responsibility. People with a sense of responsibility are more willing to take ownership.

- When you care about people, they feel secure. People who feel secure are more willing to take initiative.

- Validate everything you do from *their* perspective.

Engagement-Performance Model™

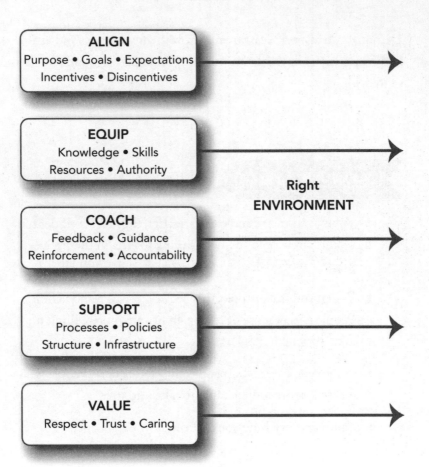

THE RIGHT ENVIRONMENT

To create the right environment, align their hearts and minds, equip them to succeed, coach them to perform, design your organization to support them, and value them as people, as individuals. Approach all of it from their perspective.

At the start of Part III, I asked you to complete the Alignment Questionnaire for leaders. Now, let's find out what your team members are experiencing. Turn over the page and you'll see the Alignment Questionnaire for team members (you can also download it: RuthlessConsistency.com; password: MakeItHappen). Give your team members three minutes to complete it . . .

How did their answers compare with yours? Are you surprised? Did they check fewer "Yes" boxes? What would be a good score for them? When they've checked every "Yes" box.

Create the right environment. Seek out, eliminate, and prevent misalignments. Verify it from *your people's* perspective.

Alignment Questionnaire—Team Members

For each of the following items, check the box that most accurately represents the truth of the statement. If an item doesn't apply, then leave it blank. Total each of the columns at the bottom of the page.

	YES		NO
STRATEGIC FOCUS Our organization has a clear and concise definition of success	☐	*If NO, then stop*	☐

THE RIGHT ENVIRONMENT	YES	SOMEWHAT	NO
1. I understand and believe in the purpose of our organization.	☐	☐	☐
2. I understand our organization's goals.	☐	☐	☐
3. I understand what is expected of me in my job.	☐	☐	☐
4. I understand how what I do supports our purpose and goals.	☐	☐	☐
5. I feel motivated to achieve what is expected.	☐	☐	☐
6. I have the skills to achieve what is expected.	☐	☐	☐
7. I have the information and knowledge to achieve what is expected.	☐	☐	☐
8. I have the resources to achieve what is expected.	☐	☐	☐
9. I have the time to achieve what is expected.	☐	☐	☐
10. I have the authority to achieve what is expected.	☐	☐	☐
11. I receive meaningful feedback about my performance.	☐	☐	☐
12. I receive guidance that helps me improve.	☐	☐	☐
13. I am reinforced for achieving what is expected.	☐	☐	☐
14. I am held accountable if I don't achieve what is expected.	☐	☐	☐
15. The right processes are in place to help me achieve what is expected.	☐	☐	☐
16. I can influence how processes are changed or improved.	☐	☐	☐
17. Our policies support my efforts to achieve what is expected.	☐	☐	☐
18. We have the right positions on the org chart to achieve what is expected.	☐	☐	☐
19. Departments and locations work effectively together to achieve what is expected.	☐	☐	☐
20. Our facilities allow me to achieve what is expected.	☐	☐	☐
21. Our equipment enables me to achieve what is expected.	☐	☐	☐
22. My manager respects me, trusts me, and cares about me as a person.	☐	☐	☐
TOTALS:	☐	☐	☐

PART IV

THE RIGHT TEAM

The best players don't always make the best team.
But the best team almost always wins.

—Coaching adage

Right focus? Check. Right environment? Check. Right team?

If everyone is engaged and performing up to expectations, then yes. If not, then you've got work to do. Without the right focus and right environment, you wouldn't have known if you had the right team. A lack of focus or a misaligned environment could have undermined their efforts. But now, with the right focus and right environment, if you have the right team, then everyone wins. If you don't have the right team . . . you'll know it.

Amira, the CEO of a building products company, knew it. After developing a Strategic Framework with her team and creating the right environment to support it, she learned that some team members were in over their heads. "It exposed the weak links in the chain," she explained, "who could execute and who couldn't. It revealed who could lead, who would take initiative, who could come up with solutions, and who was just going along for the ride."

Ruthless Consistency®

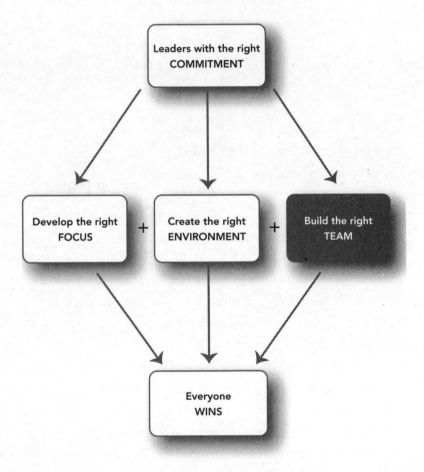

You have to have the right team. How do you build it? It comes down to processes. Yes, processes. Robust and rigorous processes for attracting strong talent and selecting the best candidates. Not necessarily the most capable *individuals*, but the most capable *team members*. Then, having a process to evaluate and strengthen those processes.

You want to be ruthlessly consistent? Focus and environment aren't enough. Build and keep rebuilding the right team.

DON'T JUST RECRUIT; COMPETE

Recruitment IS marketing.

—Matthew Jeffrey

DESPITE YOUR BEST EFFORTS, one of your team members simply isn't performing up to expectations. You need to upgrade. If you've determined there are no internal candidate who are even close to qualified, then you need to look externally.

Attracting and securing top talent is one of the biggest obstacles to your organization's ongoing success. Many organizations are finding that the standard approaches to attracting talent just aren't good enough. It's time to rethink recruitment.

Adopt this mindset, and you'll have a fighting chance:

Compete for talent.

You're no longer simply recruiting; you're competing for talent. You're not just hiring; you're competing for talent. And you'd better compete for talent as fiercely as you compete for customers, because prospective employees have choices, and they're asking the same questions as prospective customers: Why you? Why not your competitors? What makes your organization special? What's in it for me? How will you help me grow? What opportunities will you provide?

Competing for talent is about the *right mindset* and the *right methods*.

WHO: IT TAKES A TEAM TO BUILD A TEAM

Competing for talent isn't simply the responsibility of your HR department. Yes, HR plays a vital role, but your first move in competing for talent is recognizing that it's a *joint responsibility*. It takes a team to build a team.

Marketing

The first place to look beyond your HR department is your marketing department. Broaden its mandate. If you want to be a company that competes for talent, then the role of the marketing department should be expanded to helping attract prospective employees as well as prospective customers. Marketing's expertise—capturing attention, shaping perceptions, creating desire, and prompting action—is exactly what's needed to recruit and hire the best.

One example is your company's website. Compare it with your competitors' websites. Within 10 seconds, can prospective employees who visit your website find where to click to learn about careers?[1] If they can, you're off to a good start. Now, what they had better *not* see is simply a list of job openings. What you want them to see are images, videos, and copy that speak to *them*, that make an emotional connection, that make *them* feel good. Like the kind of people doing the kind of work in the kind of environment that they would like. Like being part of a winning team, a team that is admired, that has fun, and that contributes to the fabric of the community. You want them to identify with what they see and to feel like they belong.

Marketing can also play a valuable role in other recruitment efforts such as designing social media campaigns, job fair experiences, facility tours, referral programs, and publicity campaigns.

Sales

Competing for talent means that once you've attracted good candidates, you want to keep them in the evaluation funnel until *you've* made a decision. It's criminal to advance a prospective employee through to the final phase of your hiring process only to have the person leave you at the altar.

Your sales department can help. Its expertise lies in moving prospects through the sales funnel and, most importantly, closing the deal. Do you have sales trainers? Have them deliver a targeted sales training session for your recruiters. Or invite your top sales reps to share their best practices for building rapport, identifying individual needs, establishing competitive positioning, and overcoming objections. Yes, recruiters need to sell as well as evaluate. Don't leave it to chance. Keep prospective employees in the game until *you're* ready to decide.

Operations

Do you have process management expertise in your operations department? Great, because your process for evaluating and deciding on prospective team members had better not be inefficient or ineffective. If it's inefficient—slow or cumbersome—good candidates will get frustrated and take themselves out of the game. If it's ineffective, you might not be selecting the strongest candidates.

Enlist your process management experts to help design an effective and efficient evaluation and decision-making process. While they won't have "content" expertise—your HR people will—they will contribute process expertise, considering both the needs of the candidate and the needs of your organization.

The Strategic Leadership Team

Competing for talent is a strategic issue. That means it can't just be pushed down the org chart and ignored by the Strategic Leadership Team. If you're struggling to compete for talent, then make it a managed project. Develop a project plan with time-linked milestones and include it as a fixed agenda item at every Strategic Leadership Team meeting.

Each member of your Strategic Leadership Team should be on the lookout for talent. Let's say, for example, you're looking for strong customer service people. The next time you're dining in a restaurant, and your server is personable, professional, and presents well, consider the following approach, which a number of our clients have successfully applied. At the end of the meal, say something like this:

"Blair, I've really enjoyed your service tonight. I don't know what your career plans are, but if you're ever looking for a change, I'd love to speak with you about why we're a great company to work for. From what I've seen tonight, you just might be a great fit for our company. Here's my card, I'm the (your title). Feel free to contact me directly. Thanks again, Blair."

Strategic Leadership Team members are generally well connected. Have them develop a plan to reach out to professional and personal contacts, as well as the membership organizations they belong to, and then report back to the rest of the team.

All Team Members

Referral programs aren't unique, but there is a difference between those that are well designed and those that aren't. The most common mistake is paying out the full referral incentive once a new team member is hired. Far better to pay out the bulk of the incentive once a new team member has been with the company for a fixed time period, such as 90 days.

As an alternative to money, consider offering referring team members an experience or perhaps a menu of product and service options to select from.

Make it easy for team members to engage and refer prospective candidates. Equip them with information and tools to increase their confidence and skill. Bullet points that highlight how to identify and how to approach prospective candidates, how to position the company, and how to gain permission to refer them can all be helpful. However, make sure not to overwhelm them with information.

The referral process should be simple. We worked with one company that was mystified why its referral program wasn't generating any referrals. After we reviewed the referral process and interviewed a number of employees, it became clear that the process was the problem. It was cumbersome to log in and access the referral page, and too much information was required. Employees decided it just wasn't worth the effort.

It's important to regularly communicate referral metrics—goals and actuals of the number of people referred, the number hired, and the number retained after 90 days. It's also important to communicate and promote what employees received for providing referrals—the amount of money paid out or the number and types of experiences and gifts.

WHAT: THINK *CAPABILITIES*, NOT JUST EMPLOYEES

Your organization is growing. To keep up with the demands of growth, you need to hire more employees.

Or do you? Acquiring the capabilities you need doesn't necessarily mean hiring employees. Capabilities come in many forms: full-time, part-time, permanent, temporary, employment, contract, and even volunteer.

The first question to ask is what additional capabilities does your organization need to win? Next, do those capabilities exist internally? If not, can you develop them within a reasonable time at an acceptable cost? If the answer is no, then look externally. Does fulfilling the capabilities justify an employment position, or is it more time and cost effective to bring in a consultant or contract person? If it justifies employment, is it an ongoing need or a temporary one? And does the need require a full-time commitment?

As the workforce changes, now more than ever you need to evolve your mindset from *we need more employees* to *we need the right capabilities*.

HOW: TACTICS TO COMPETE AND WIN

How can your organization compete for talent? Here are four ways.

Develop Relationships

One of our clients was struggling, trying to attract talented engineers. To compete for talent, we decided they should form "deep relationships" with the local university. It started with a well-managed internship program, followed by targeted scholarships, but what took it to a deeper level was sponsoring an annual competition. The company posed an engineering problem to the school, provided funding for teams, arranged for students to receive course credit, and then hosted a presentations-and-awards banquet. *Oh, and while you're here, let us show you our facilities, the interesting work we do, the great people employed here, and our fun and fulfilling environment . . .*

Do you think that helped them attract engineers? Absolutely.

Increasingly, companies are competing for talent by hosting events that interest prospective recruits. In the high-tech world, for example, hackathons provide forums to engage people, have fun, and create positive impressions about a company and its culture.

Know your target audience, and design events that appeal to their interests, both work related and personal.

Look for the Opportunities in the Obstacles

A long-term employee says she plans to retire. The company throws a retirement party. The employee leaves.

Or . . . a long-term employee says she plans to retire. The company says, "We'd love to have you stay with us part-time. That will allow you more time with the grandkids *and* help to pay for those trips you've been talking about." The employee stays.

Your longer-term employees may not realize that there's an alternative to going from full-time work to full-time retirement. For some, ongoing part-time work can offer the best of both worlds. Keep in mind that fewer people are taking a "hard" retirement. Many want to stay active and keep working, at least part-time, to meet their social, financial, and self-fulfillment needs.

Changing workforce trends provide you with opportunities, not just obstacles. The growth of the gig economy and the desire for more flexible and varied work schedules are examples of other trends. Can you take advantage of these to meet your capabilities needs?

Uhhh, About Your Hiring Standards . . .

This one might hurt a bit, but at the very least you need to consider it.

Lower your hiring standards. What? Yes, lower your hiring standards . . . but do it selectively. Remember the old adage, "Hire for attitude, train for skill"? Sometimes, it's a necessity. If there simply aren't enough candidates with the skills you need, then you may have to invest more in developing those skills. Selectively lowering your hiring standards expands your selection pool and helps attract people who see that you're willing to invest in them.

Which standards should you lower? Make sure not to lower your performance standards. And *never* compromise your organization's values or the individual traits that are critical to success. But you may want to reconsider your requirements for education, experience, and skills. Are your educational requirements nice-to-haves or must-haves? Does the successful candidate really need so many years of experience, or could you compensate for a lack of experience with mentoring, coaching, or pairing the new team member with a high-performing peer? And instead of requiring certain skills, could you develop them? "Ah," you might be thinking, "but what if we train them and they leave?" If you think that's bad, what if you don't train them and they stay? As Richard Branson, founder of the Virgin Group, once said, "Train people well enough so they can leave, treat them well enough so they don't want to."[2]

Design a Compelling Prospect Experience

You know it's important to deliver a compelling customer experience. It's just as important to deliver a compelling *prospect experience*. Every touchpoint with prospective candidates—from the first impression through to their hire—should be managed: (1) to create a sense of purpose and belonging, (2) to have them feel good about your company and your people, and (3) to advance them through the process.

Start by making it quick and easy for prospective employees to contact you through the channel of their choice (e.g., social media, text, web, email, etc.). When they do reach out, respond quickly and with positive energy. Every communication that follows should be clear, engaging, and timely; every interaction, warm and personable.

When you invite a candidate in for an interview, put out a welcome sign with the person's name on it. Have your receptionist come out and provide a warm welcome. Determine in advance the candidate's preferred workplace beverage and have it waiting in the interview room.

Connect with the heart, and the head will follow. Make sure the candidate gets a *feel* for your company, your people, and your culture. Have the person meet with employees with whom they can identify, people who engage with genuine interest and positive energy. Make sure your people are prepped to greet and interact with the candidate.

Paint a picture. Let them know how they can play a critical role in your company and the kinds of career paths that would be available to them.

Use speed to your advantage. Companies that treat the hiring process with urgency are not only quick to identify and pursue the best talent; they send the message that they're on a mission and driven to succeed.

For example, software company Intuit has candidates go through an intensive series of interviews and evaluations in a single day. Intuit employees play a major role in the process. At the end of the day, the evaluation team makes decisions and will often give successful candidates same-day offers.

Are you using speed to your advantage? If you don't act with urgency in your hiring process, your competitors will.

TAKEAWAYS

- Leverage the expertise of marketing, sales, and operations to strengthen your recruitment process.

- Have your Strategic Leadership Team members tap into their networks to source potential team members.

- Involve all your employees by implementing a well-designed referral program.

- Design your recruitment process so that every touchpoint creates a positive emotional connection with prospective employees.

- Start now. Prospective employees are considering your competitors *as you're reading this*. Compete for talent!

HIRE FOR WHAT YOU'RE LIKELY TO OVERLOOK

Talent is good. Practice is better. Passion is best.

—Frank Lloyd Wright

YOU'VE ATTRACTED A SOLID POOL of job candidates. Now, *what* should you look for in selecting the top candidate?

Most companies focus on job-specific skills and experience. Can the person do the job? Has the person done the job? Some dig deeper; they try to determine the person's values. Skills, experience, and values—all very important. But a candidate could check all those boxes yet still disappoint you, because there's one more category that strongly predicts success. And you're likely to overlook it.

Theo Epstein was a pioneer of the analytics movement in baseball, which brought greater sophistication to player evaluation and selection. As general manager of the Boston Red Sox, his methods helped the team break an 86-year "curse" and win the World Series. Then they won it a second time.

At the end of Epstein's final season in Boston, the talent-laden Red Sox melted down and missed the playoffs. Analyzing why, he came to a realization that changed his thinking about player selection: *Skills and experience weren't enough.* To deal with the pressures and ups and downs of a long and grueling season, he needed players who possessed something he had previously overlooked. *The right traits.* One trait that was especially relevant, given the Red Sox recent meltdown, was the drive to overcome adversity. That's because overcoming adversity reflects a tenacity that correlates well with winning. As a result, Epstein made the evaluation of traits a core part of his player selection process.

Epstein went on to become President of Baseball Operations for the Chicago Cubs. Four seasons later, after applying his revised methods, the Cubs ended *their* drought of 108 years and won the World Series.

WHAT TRAITS CAN TELL YOU

Traits are personal qualities and characteristics that can tell you a lot about how people will function in the workplace. For example, will they go above and beyond, or will they do the bare minimum? Will they put the team's interests first or their own? Will they take initiative or wait to be told what to do?

Suppose you're hiring an early-career professional, someone who has a solid education but who's short on skills and experience. Which fundamental traits should you look for? Studying early-career professionals in our clients' companies, we've found that certain traits correlate well with success:

1. Punctual—early or on-time

2. Prepared—ready and equipped

3. Engaged—100 percent focused on whatever they're doing

4. Reliable—do what they say they're going to do

5. Respectful—of everyone, all the time

6. Positive—see the possibilities, opportunities, and upsides

7. Inquisitive—strive to learn and grow

8. Coachable—open to constructive feedback and guidance

9. Driven—have a desire to achieve and succeed

10. Forward-looking—anticipate and solve problems

Skills tell you what a candidate *can do*. Experience tells you what a candidate *has done*. Values tell you what a candidate *wants to do*. Traits tell you what a candidate *will do*.

TRAITS THAT FIT YOUR STRATEGY

Imagine your strategy is to consistently provide impeccable retail service. Which traits should you look for when hiring people? Consider John Jaster. John is the managing director at Andrisen Morton, a men's fine clothing retailer in Denver. A few years back, I was having a new jacket made on short notice. I had planned to fly out of Denver early on a Monday morning, and the jacket wasn't going to be ready until late the Saturday before, which meant I was out of luck if any alterations had to be made. Not a problem, I thought. The store's got my measurements nailed down. But that wasn't good enough for John.

"Why don't I come in and meet you on Sunday?" he said. *Sunday?* John wanted to make sure my new jacket fit perfectly, so of course he offered to come in on his day off. It was automatic. He didn't have to think about it, and he didn't make a pretend offer, hoping I would say no. It's who he is. Impeccable service.

On another occasion, I asked him about his philosophy of service. "When someone comes into our store," he explained, "I feel like I'm welcoming them into my home. They're a guest. I want them to relax.

"We're not selling," he continued. "We're providing a service. It's the things our parents taught us: politeness, manners. It's what I always emphasize with our new staff. When a person walks in the store, if your mindset is that you're going to sell something, then this isn't the place for you."

What about challenging customers? We've all experienced them.

"Empathy," he said without missing a beat. "I learned from my dad that you never know what a person is experiencing or what they've gone through. You have to remember it's about them; it's not about you. You can't go wrong with empathy."

I thanked John for his insights. "Hey, any time," he replied. "Just let me know whenever you need me. Even if it's midnight, I can come into the store."

Putting the needs of others first, making them feel like guests, politeness, empathy, flexibility—traits that are critical to consistently providing impeccable service. Does it make a difference? Absolutely. It's why I've been a customer of John's for over 15 years.

Now imagine your strategy is to create a culture of innovation in which everyone looks for ways to help your company improve and evolve. Which traits should you look for? Consider Momofuku Ando. On a biting cold night in 1957, Ando was walking home from the salt-making factory in Osaka, Japan. He saw clouds of steam in the street around which a crowd of people were huddled. They were waiting, a long time as it turned out, for noodles to be cooked in vats of boiling water. "Why should they wait so long?" he thought.

He quickly become consumed with the challenge of making noodles that didn't take so long to cook. After a year of trial and error in his backyard shed, Ando discovered the secret of revitalizing precooked noodles that were flavorful. "Instant noodles" were born. In 1958 he sold 13 million bags of his three-minute noodles. Today, over 100 billion servings of instant noodles are eaten around the world each year. The Japanese voted instant noodles their second most important invention of the twentieth century after the (now obsolete) Sony Walkman.

Innovation is rooted in four traits: a *dissatisfaction* with how things are, the *inquisitiveness* to ponder "what if," a *bias for action*, and the *persistence* to transform the what-if into a viable reality. All four are essential. Dissatisfaction alone results in frustration and complaining. Add inquisitiveness, and you're still only daydreaming. Taking action gets you in the game, yet add persistence and now you have what separates true innovators from mere dabblers. How persistent is persistent? As one example, James Dyson, the inventor and founder of Dyson vacuums, went through *5,127 prototypes* of his dual-cyclone, bagless vacuum cleaner before launching it to the market. *That's* persistence.

TRAITS THAT FIT THE SITUATION

We worked with a company in the building products industry that was hiring a VP of marketing. It came down to two candidates, both of whom had the required skills and experience. Yet one of the candidates was a natural fit with the company culture while the other was somewhat of a stretch. Which one would you choose?

Not so fast. Hiring for fit with your current culture reinforces that culture. But what if you need to *evolve* your culture? What if your people need to think and act differently? Then you should hire for fit with the *desired culture*. The traits you select for need to fit the situation.

That was our client's situation, and that's what he did. He selected the candidate who would help shift the culture. A *constructive agitator* who would inject some discomfort into the status quo. (We of course reminded the CEO that cultures can only process so much change so fast. A constructive agitator not sensitive to that could become marginalized or might even trigger a culture war.)

Context counts. If you're operating in a fast-changing environment, you want people who are adaptable. If performance expectations in your industry are ever-rising, you want people who are driven to learn and improve. If you have a distributed workforce with minimal supervision, you want people with a strong sense of responsibility who take initiative.

You don't necessarily want all your team members to have the same traits. Sometimes, it's important they have complementary traits. That can even be true at the top of your organization with the CEO and COO or the CEO and CFO. My favorite example is Soichiro Honda and Takeo Fujisawa. Honda was a mechanic and engineer who was fascinated with engines, design, and technology. He was a tireless worker and an intense perfectionist. He was also prone to emotional outbursts, and was called *Kaminari-san*—Mr. Thunder—for his temper when others failed to meet his performance standards.

Takeo Fujisawa was the calm to Honda's storm. A skilled administrator with expertise in marketing and finance, Fujisawa was less intense than Honda and could see the gray where his colleague could only see black and white. He would counsel people, not yell at them. Honda and Fujisawa were perfect complements, and together they built the largest motorcycle company in the world in just over 10 years. (You may have heard they later expanded into automobiles.)

How can leaders with such different traits work so effectively together? First, they were both *self-aware* (another important trait). Each had great confidence in his abilities yet was well aware of his limitations. Second, they had tremendous *respect for and trust in* each other's capabilities. Third, they shared a *common vision*: to build a thriving, global company committed to innovation.

It's not critical that each member of your team has every required trait; it's critical that your team *collectively* has the required traits. Don't just hire people like you; hire people who complement you.

THE SEARCH FOR UNIVERSAL SUCCESS TRAITS

Aside from the traits that fit your strategy or a specific situation, are there traits you should look for in every new hire? While there are many tools used to assess traits along a variety of dimensions—DISC, Myers-Briggs Type Indicator, Predictive Index, and Culture Index being common examples—they aren't designed as general predictors of workplace success.

Ian MacRae and Adrian Furnham at University College London have identified and extensively validated six traits that are consistently linked to workplace success and that make up their *High Potential Trait Indicator (HPTI):*[1]

Conscientiousness. People who are conscientious take ownership of their responsibilities, decisions, and actions. They commit to following through. They don't succumb to impatience or the urge to just get by.

Curiosity. Curious people like to get to the root causes of issues, which in turn helps them learn. They like to imagine possibilities that can lead to innovations.

Courage. Courageous people are willing to think independently and to take risks. For anyone in a leadership role, especially, taking well-conceived risks is essential.

Competitiveness. People who are competitive are motivated, not necessarily to beat others, but to excel and succeed. They push themselves. They're not easily discouraged by setbacks or adversity.

Adjustment. Well-adjusted people deal well with pressure and stress. They frame these in a more positive way (or at least less negative way) than less well-adjusted people. They don't let anxieties get the best of them.

Ambiguity tolerance. People with this trait are comfortable with uncertainty. They are open to the merits of different perspectives. They are not only more adaptive to change, but quicker to adapt.

This research has been validated across various business sectors over a number of years. MacRae rightly cautions, however, that any of the traits taken to an extreme could be problematic. Excessive curiosity, for example, could lead to endless contemplation while little-or-nothing gets done. As a result, he and Furnham identified four ranges along the scale for each trait: low, moderate, optimal, and excessive. Those most likely to succeed have traits in the optimal range.

TWO MINDSETS

Carol Dweck is a Stanford psychologist who studies human motivation and achievement. At the heart of her thinking is the idea that there are two mindsets: a *fixed* mindset and a *growth* mindset.[2] Dweck's research looks at how the mindset we adopt fundamentally shapes our lives.

Essentially, fixed-mindset people believe that their capabilities are locked in. They say things such as "I'm not good at math" or "I dropped the plate because I always do that." People with a growth mindset believe that capabilities are subject to change. They make comments such as "I can get better at math" or "I dropped the plate because I wasn't paying attention."

A fixed mindset is *deterministic*: We perform at a certain level because that's who we are. It doesn't allow for learning or improvement. A growth mindset is *dynamic*: We can perform better because we have the capacity to learn, grow, and improve.

In general, you want to hire team members who have more of a growth mindset. Yet what if some of your current team members don't have that mindset? Fortunately, you can help shift their thinking. One approach is to set expectations that stretch them just outside of their comfort zones, provide ample encouragement and support, and then reinforce and celebrate improvements. Over time, they'll gain confidence and comfort in stretching themselves, and adopt more of a growth mindset.

WHAT ELSE YOU'RE LIKELY
TO OVERLOOK . . .

At the beginning of the chapter, I said that job-related skills and experience weren't enough, that a person's traits, which are often overlooked, are important in predicting success. Yet what about indirect skills and experiences? Could those be relevant and help to predict success?

Self-Management Skills

Let's say you're evaluating a candidate to fill a key management position. You're likely to assume something that shouldn't be assumed—that the candidate can self-manage, that she has an effective system for capturing and recording tasks and commitments, for organizing, prioritizing, and scheduling them, and then for managing them through to completion. Surprisingly, many managers lack these seemingly basic skills. Yet it's easy for you to take them for granted. Don't.

Life Experiences

Life experiences can be relevant to a job. If, for example, you were interviewing a single mom who raised three kids while getting her degree and working full-time, what would that tell you? That she is motivated, hardworking, and able to juggle and prioritize competing demands. That might be very relevant to the job for which you're hiring.

Sometimes, it's not obvious how non-job-related experiences might apply. Imagine you're a partner in a law firm that's hiring new lawyers. Are there experiences that might hint at the likelihood of a successful hire? It was a question I asked Tim, my lawyer, one morning over breakfast.

"I like it if they've been a waiter," he said without pausing. *What?* "If they've worked in that kind of job, then they're used to a stressful environment. They've learned the importance of teamwork, and they're continually dealing with customer relations. And they're likely to be trustworthy because they're dealing with money."

Well, who would have thought?

Many companies like to hire former athletes, those who played competitive sports at a high level. The assumption is that they understand what it means to intensively pursue a goal, to work hard at improving, and to deal with adversity. But are those assumptions true? The first thing I want to know is whether the former athlete was a "natural" or a "worker." Naturals may have gotten by based on ability alone. That ability might have masked poor work habits or less-than-maximum effort. Workers, on the other hand, were often overachievers—highly motivated individuals who trained exceptionally hard.

Next, I want to know what the former athlete achieved. Did she progress from being on the second team to becoming a starter? From being a starter to an all-star? Was she happy just being on the team, or did she strive to improve and excel? Was she a team captain?

Then, I want to know how she dealt with the inevitable defeats, setbacks, and injuries—emotionally, intellectually, and behaviorally. In short, I want to know how she dealt with adversity. Because in the working world she's going to face lots of it.

Did she play a team or individual sport? In general, team sport athletes understand the importance of teamwork in achieving success. They know what it means to sacrifice for the good of the team, and they enjoy the camaraderie and team spirit. On the other hand, individual sport athletes tend to be self-motivated and self-reliant. They are often well organized and good at time and activity management. And they've been trained to objectively analyze their strengths, limitations, and performance.

While the background of former athletes often transfers well to business, make sure to test your assumptions by probing the specifics of their competitive experience.

Finally, recognize that competitive experience can be gained in many fields: the performing arts, gaming, adventure activities—it doesn't matter. You're looking for a *competitive spirit*, not just a competitive background—a spirit that keeps driving the person to excel, to improve, and to win.

> *You're looking for a competitive spirit, not just a competitive background.*

THE ONE TRAIT THAT IGNITES EVERYTHING

The next time you're in Cleveland, you must—*must*—dine at Mallorca. Not because of the delectable Spanish- and Portuguese-inspired cuisine. Because of Enrique.

Tall and lean with Latin features, Enrique the server has an unparalleled passion for his profession. My first time at Mallorca he asked me about my appetizer, which was conversation-stopping good. "That was *very* tasty," I exclaimed.

He slowly leaned forward, a fire building inside, and with barely restrained intensity said, "The best . . . is yet . . . to come!" Then he was off. I was stunned. But he was absolutely right.

A few years later I returned with my wife and our Cleveland friends, unsure of what we might experience, wanting to hope, but not too much, knowing that such experiences are rarely repeated. Of course, we asked for Enrique. As he started describing the specials, *it* happened. I could see the fire building again. "Tonight . . . the baby . . . goat! You know, the little ones, they don't get away so easy!" He continued, the shackles on his intensity breaking away. "We have seared . . . tuna! It melts in your mouth like butter! And a wonderful salmon . . . topped with garlic shrimp!" Finally, he gave in. "Give me those!" he cried out, snatching the menus from our hands. "You don't need them! Tonight . . . I am the menu!" And then he was off. That was that. We had no idea what we'd be eating or how much it would cost. *And it didn't matter!*

All of us love to be around people who so openly love what they do. Passion is the trait that ignites everything else.

What would happen if your organization had 50 Enriques? What stories would your customers tell?

TAKEAWAYS

- When assessing potential employees, look for skills, experience, values, and especially, traits.

- Well-validated research (the HPTI) has identified six traits that, at optimal levels, correlate very well with workplace success: conscientiousness, curiosity, courage, competitiveness, adjustment, and ambiguity tolerance.

- Look for traits that support your specific strategy or situation.

- Look for people with a *growth* mindset, those who believe they can learn, grow, and improve.

- Consider non-job-specific skills and life experiences that might relate to the position you're filling.

- Passion is the trait that ignites everything else. Hire people who have a natural passion for the job.

BE SELECTIVE IN HOW YOU SELECT

People are not your most important asset.
The right people are.

—Jim Collins

HOW DO YOU EFFECTIVELY ASSESS a job candidate? Do you conduct a couple of interviews? Call a reference or two? Do you even have a consistent and documented assessment process?

If you're just looking for a warm body, then do a pulse check, and if you feel something, give the person the job. But if building the right team is critical to your success, then you'd better have an *effective*, *efficient*, and *evolving* selection process. How confident are you that your current selection process meets those criteria?

CONVERGING EVIDENCE: HOW TO SELECT

Which assessment method can give you the confidence that you're selecting the best candidate? The reality is, no one method can do

Converging Evidence

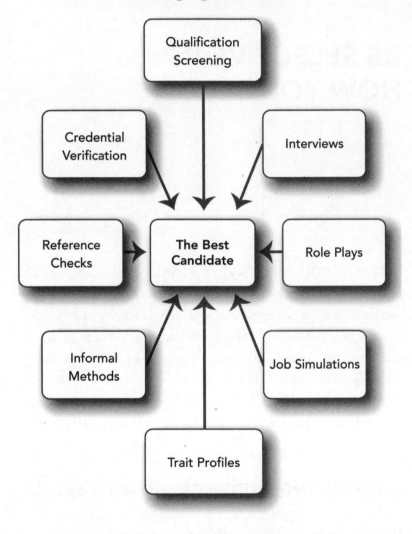

that. Look for *converging evidence*. The more that evidence from different methods converges on the same conclusion, the more confident you can be in that conclusion.

Start by identifying the assessment methods that are most relevant for the position.

1. Qualification Screening

First, you need to identify what success looks like for the position you're filling, and then you need to determine the basic requirements for success (skills, experience, values, and traits). This can help with the initial qualification screening.

Don't erect false barriers. Distinguish between must-haves, should-haves, and nice-to-haves. A common barrier that companies erect is the education barrier—requiring that a candidate has a degree or advanced degree. Don't get me wrong; I'm all for education. But organizations shouldn't identify having a degree as a hard-and-fast job requirement if it's not.

The best boss I ever had was Arthur Stanley at FedEx. Arthur was focused, bright, and committed. He cared about his people and had impeccable integrity. He gave us direction and support and then let us do our jobs. He recognized our accomplishments and held us constructively accountable. Arthur got results. He had a successful career as an executive both domestically and internationally.

What Arthur didn't have was a university degree. If that had been a barrier, then FedEx—and everyone on Arthur's team including me—would never have benefited from his leadership.

Say that a degree is preferred. Say that it's *strongly* preferred. But unless it's absolutely necessary—meaning a person *can't* do the job without it—don't make it a barrier.

2. Interviews

One interview conducted by one person isn't going to tell you a lot. You want multiple interviews conducted by various people, including the candidate's future boss, peers, and, if applicable, direct reports. While interviewing is important, it's also easy to do poorly. Here are some landmines to avoid:

Don't just ask hypothetical, "What would you do if . . . ?" questions. Hypothetical questions lead to hypothetical answers. Better to ask real-world questions. *Behavior-based interviewing* involves asking candidates for examples of how they dealt with specific situations that relate to the job. For example, "Tell me about a time when a customer made a reasonable request that went outside of company policy. What did you do and why? What was the outcome?"

Do you remember how Theo Epstein of the Chicago Cubs identified "overcoming adversity" as a critical trait? He assessed that through behavior-based interviewing. He would ask prospective players for three examples of when they overcame adversity outside of baseball, as well as three baseball-related examples.

Don't focus exclusively on results. Results are important but can be hugely misleading. Let's say a candidate for a sales manager position oversaw sales growth of 75 percent over three years in her previous job. Sounds impressive, right? Maybe not. Did the results happen because of her or despite her? Did she spearhead the effort, was she a contributor, or was she simply an innocent bystander, the beneficiary of economic, market, or industry conditions? Specifically, what was her plan to grow sales? Who developed it and how? What specific actions did she take? Why? What challenges did she face, and how did she deal with them? Make sure not to accept answers that begin with "our" or "we." They could be a mask for what her team did or what higher-ups told her to do, not what *she* actually did.

Don't be predictable. Job interviews are like theater. Each person has a role, prepares for it, and takes the "stage" to play it. To position themselves as the ideal candidate, many interviewees become skilled actors, anticipating questions and providing answers that make them appear—take your pick—confident/humble/successful/experienced/driven/creative/friendly.

Rip the script. Break the candidates out of their rehearsed role. As a start, here are five interview questions (and follow-up questions) they won't expect:

1. Describe the culture of a company in which you would be a poor fit. (Why would you be a poor fit?)

2. What's the biggest misconception people have about you? (Why would they have that misconception?)

3. What's a little-known fact that people would be surprised to learn about you? (Why would it surprise them?)

4. What have you intentionally done to learn and grow over the past year? (Why did you specifically choose that?)

5. What's one of your life ambitions? (What steps have you taken towards achieving it?)

The answers won't tell you whether the person is the ideal candidate, but they will help you assess the real candidate.

3. Role Plays

When a position you're hiring for requires strong interpersonal skills, such as sales or customer service, role plays can be helpful. Instead of asking a potential customer service rep to *explain* how he's handled an upset customer, have him role-play the situation. (Make sure you give him sufficient context to conduct a meaningful role play.) It allows you to observe his skill at thinking on his feet, in deciding what to say and how to say it. It also helps you assess traits such as empathy and patience.

Similarly, if you want to know how a potential sales rep would overcome customer objections or how a potential manager would coach an underperforming employee, conduct a role play and have him *show* you what he would do, not just tell you what he would do.

4. Job Simulations

If you're hiring for technical skills, consider having the candidate demonstrate them. Hiring a new CFO? While a candidate might look good on paper, you want to know how analytical she is. Put her in a room with a set of mock financial statements for a fixed time. Then have her present her assessment, pose questions, and make recommendations.

If dealing with pressure and being able to multitask are critical job requirements, then devise a simulation in which the candidate is hit with multiple demands and given insufficient time to process them. If making presentations is critical to the role, then have the candidate give a presentation to your team.

Like role plays, the benefit of job simulations is they require candidates to *show* you, not simply tell you.

5. Trait Profiles

Trait profiles can provide you with insights into a candidate that might be hard to determine from an interview. How conscientious is the person? Does the person prefer a more-structured or less-structured environment? How patient is the person? Is the person a more dominant or less dominant type?

Many instruments are available to help assess a candidate's traits, such as the HPTI outlined in the last chapter, as well as DISC, Myers-Briggs Type Indicator, Predictive Index, and Culture Index. Many successful companies we've worked with wouldn't think of hiring for a key position without first assessing the candidate's trait profile.

6. Informal Methods

I had flown into Atlanta to interview for an executive consultant position with The Atlanta Consulting Group. The firm had a driver pick me up at the airport. On the way into the office, we had a pleasant conversation about the driver's limo business, life in Atlanta, the local sports teams, and similar subjects.

After I got the job, I learned something that surprised me. My ride with the driver was part of the assessment process. His role was to find out what kind of person I was. Engaging or reserved? Professional or casual? Respectful or patronizing? He knew the people and the culture at the firm. Would I be a good fit?

Consider other informal methods for evaluating job candidates such as the casual probings of your receptionist or an informal social gathering with members of your team. Of course, online searches can provide a world of insights.

When hiring for key positions, find opportunities to evaluate job candidates outside of the formal evaluation process.

7. Reference Checks

Unfortunately, because of legal concerns and respondent biases, reference checks are generally not that helpful. At a minimum, they can help verify a candidate's employment history. Ideally, they would speak to the candidate's performance and offer insights into the person's skills and traits.

Asking nonstandard questions is more likely to provoke thoughtful answers: What is one thing about Penny that's likely to surprise us? What is Ty's strongest trait? If there's one thing we need to watch with Maureen, what would that be? Which three words would you use to describe Diego as a person? At best, you might uncover a few nuggets that will assist in your hiring decision.

8. Credential Verification

If a successful job candidate legitimately needs an important credential—a degree or certification, for example—it's best to have the person provide verification of it. Because every now and then job candidates will claim to have earned a credential they haven't.

Beware of Biases

I benefited from my association with FedEx for years after I had left. Because FedEx was a well-regarded company, people made assumptions about me that were positive. Yet for all they knew, I could have been lazy and incompetent.

I've known people with MBAs from famous universities who weren't very bright, people who worked for admired companies yet weren't competent, and people with big titles on their résumés who accomplished little. I've also known people with MBAs from lesser-known universities who were very bright, people who worked with unremarkable companies yet were extremely competent, and people with modest titles who accomplished much.

Don't impress easily. After you peel back the so-called credentials—degrees, company names, and titles—it comes down to the people: who are they, what have they done, what are they capable of, and what are they likely to do?

All of us make assumptions that are subject to biases. Beware. Biases can subtly contaminate your selection process.

The more that evidence from different methods converges on the same conclusion, the more confident you can be in that conclusion.

Of course, not every organization applies a multitude of methods ...

A UNIQUE APPROACH TO SELECTION

The *Berlin Philharmonic* is undoubtedly among the top symphony orchestras in the world. It has a long and storied history, with names such as Brahms, Strauss, and Grieg having served as guest conductor. In the past 75 years, the orchestra has had only six principal conductors, so the selection of a new principal is always a highly anticipated and critically important process. Given the significance of the decision, who do you think would be entrusted to make it?

The orchestra. The tenured members of the orchestra meet in a secret location—without access to cell phones or the outside world—and vote. They can vote for any conductor on the planet, yet, as a practical matter, several front-runners typically emerge based on talent, temperament, musical approach, career stage, and interest in the position. After several rounds of voting the members reach a consensus.

Should an organization of high-performing employees be able to select their leader? Given a unique set of assumptions, the answer may be "yes." If there is a strong motivation to sustain organizational excellence, a high degree of interdependence, and a recognition that sustained excellence depends on a highly capable leader who can work well with and get the most from a group of skilled performers, then yes, this can be an effective model.

Even if these assumptions aren't entirely true for your organization, should employees have a say, if not an outright vote, in the selection of the person who will be leading them? If not, why not?

ATTACK THE PROCESS: HOW TO SELECT BETTER

Once you've made your hiring decision and the new employee is established, there are three more questions you'll want to answer: (1) How successful is the person at their job? (2) How effective was your selection process? (3) How would you know?

Attack your selection process. Identify the weaknesses, gaps, and opportunities for improvement so you can continually make better hiring decisions.

Conduct an "Entry Interview"

An entry interview can provide you with valuable feedback about your selection process. Meet with each new employee in their first 30 days to get feedback about your selection process. Let the employee know your goal is to improve the selection process and that their feedback can help. Provide the employee with the following questions in advance:

1. What was most effective about our selection process?

2. What was least effective?

3. Was there anything we didn't ask or assess yet should have?

4. Was there anything we did ask or assess that wasn't relevant?

5. What did you like about the process?

6. What didn't you like about the process?

7. What is one thing we can do to make our selection process more effective?

This feedback exercise can provide helpful information to strengthen your selection process.

Conduct a 180-Day Assessment

After the employee has been with you for six months (some companies might prefer three months), bring the selection committee back together to assess the employee's performance and conduct versus what was predicted from the selection process. Ask these questions:

1. What, if anything, has surprised us about the employee's performance?

2. What, if anything, has surprised us about the employee's conduct?

3. Is there anything we didn't assess yet should have?

4. Is there anything we assessed but not as effectively as we should have?

5. Is there anything we assessed that isn't useful?

6. What are the top three things we can do to make our selection process more effective?

7. How can we accelerate the process and make it more efficient?

Whenever you hire an employee, you're essentially making a prediction about the person's performance and conduct. Feedback loops, as outlined above, can tell you how accurate your prediction was and how to improve your selection process to make better predictions.

ASSESS YOUR FAILURES

What if you need to replace a current team member who isn't meeting expectations? Don't wait until you hire the next person to assess your selection process. Go back and assess the process you used to select that person who isn't meeting expectations. Ask the same questions that make up the 180-day assessment. Use the answers to modify your process for selecting the person's replacement.

TAKEAWAYS

- Look for *converging evidence* when making hiring decisions. Employ a range of assessment methods including:

  - Qualification screening

  - Interviews

  - Role plays

  - Job simulations

  - Trait profiles

  - Informal methods

  - Reference checks

  - Credential verification

- Beware of biases that can contaminate the selection process.

- Assess your selection process *after* you hire each new team member. Meet with the person to get feedback about the process.

- After 180 days, have the selection committee come back together to assess the selection process based on the person's performance and conduct. Revise the process to make it more robust.

- Assess your previous selection process when replacing a team member who isn't meeting expectations. Use your findings to modify the process for selecting the person's replacement.

PART V

THE RIGHT COMMITMENT

To move the world, we must first move ourselves.

—Socrates

Right focus, right environment, and right team—that's what it takes to win. But it's all theoretical unless you embody the motive force that drives it: the right commitment.

At first glance it seems easy enough. Be committed. Of course, it's not so easy. There are enemies conspiring against your commitment. Fortunately, you're able to confront them. They're in the mirror.

Everything you do to develop the right focus, create the right environment, and build the right team is wasted unless *you* personify the right commitment.

Ruthless Consistency®

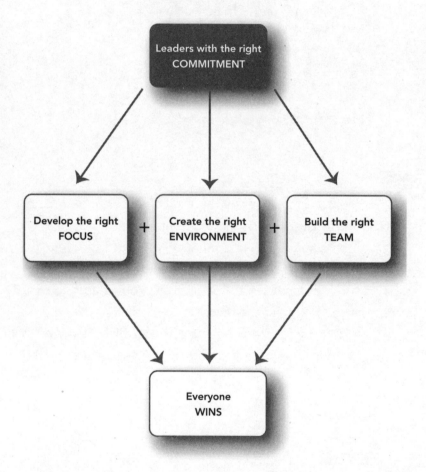

THE FIRST ENEMY YOU MUST DEFEAT

Comfort is the enemy of achievement.

—Farrah Gray

YOU'RE SUCCESSFUL. You're in the position you're in because you've achieved. Yet over time, the fire of ambition starts to lose some of its crackle. It's natural.

As a committed leader, the first enemy you must defeat is complacency. Yours.

ALWAYS HAVE AN INSPIRING NEXT GOAL

Karl Lagerfeld was an icon in the world of fashion. Creative director at Chanel for over 35 years, Fendi for over 50 years (!), as well as his own fashion house, Lagerfeld was still at the leading edge of fashion when he passed at the age of 85.

How? How is it that in a notoriously fickle industry where the creations of one season become old news almost from the moment they hit the store racks, Lagerfeld remained at the forefront and was never viewed as—perish the thought!—yesterday's man?

First, despite his countless designs, innovations, and accolades, he was unattached to and unsentimental about the past. He was forward-looking to the extreme—the next season, the next design challenge, the next show. As a writer in the *Financial Times* once noted, "For Lagerfeld, nostalgia is creative poison."[1]

In his own words, "I'm always into the next step. I'm interested in what's going on, not what has happened. I never look at the archives. I hate archives!"[2]

Second, his work was his passion, and he relentlessly immersed himself in it. On one occasion, when in his 80s, Lagerfeld staged two couture shows in Paris—one for Chanel, one for Fendi—in a single week. In the world of fashion that is a Herculean task. Clearly, Lagerfeld was not someone who was simply riding out the wave.

Are you constantly looking forward? Is your work your passion? Are you immersed in it? People who don't just achieve success but *sustain* success always have an inspiring next goal.

CREATE A PERSONAL CASE FOR CHANGE

In Chapter 5 I made the case that organizational complacency is the narcotic that dulls the drive for change. To overcome it requires a compelling Case for Change that articulates both the pain of failure and the gain of success.

The same applies to you. Be honest with yourself. Have you gotten a little complacent? More than a little? Maybe it's the past successes—you feel like you've got it figured out. Maybe it's the ornaments of success—money, objects, reputation, power. Or maybe you're just comfortable.

All of these can dampen the drive to change.

Develop a Personal Case for Change, a case compelling enough to ensure you're ruthlessly consistent in developing and sustaining the right focus, creating and re-creating the right environment, and building and rebuilding the right team.

First, determine what *you* need to do differently to drive strategic change in your organization. Do you need to align purpose and goals with individual expectations? Do you need to provide targeted resources? Do you need to hold your team constructively accountable?

Next, document both the pain that will result if you don't do what you need to do and the gain that will result if you do. Here's an example:

> If I don't create an environment that is intensely focused on the customer experience, then my team will feel frustrated, and we will continue to disappoint and lose customers.
>
> If I create an environment that is intensely focused on the customer experience, then my team will feel energized, and we will delight and retain our customers.

Or how about a Case for Change that speaks to your identity:

> If I am not ruthlessly consistent in supporting our SCIs, then my legacy will be one of failure.
>
> If I am ruthlessly consistent in supporting our SCIs, then my legacy will be one of success.

Make your Personal Case for Change visible and review it daily. Let the contrast between failure and success smolder in your psyche.

DEVELOP POWERFUL, POSITIVE PATTERNS

If you've identified your inspiring next goal and created a Personal Case for Change, now you need to convert intention into action.

Do what successful leaders in all fields do: Develop *powerful, positive patterns*. Such as a "night-before" routine. At FedEx we would often say that the success of each day starts the night before. Because delivering packages to the right location by the right time required them to be picked-up, processed, and transported correctly the previous day and night. Similarly, many successful leaders block time in their evenings to review their day, identify top priorities for the next day, schedule them, and then adhere to a lights-out time.

Another powerful pattern is to establish a morning routine. That might include when you wake up and your first few activities. Many leaders start their day with exercise. A surprising number meditate.[3] Some review their personal and professional objectives and goals. Prolific leadership author John Maxwell wakes up every morning at 5:00 and is writing by 5:30. What you do is important, but more important is that whatever you choose to do you do consistently.

Elements of routine could continue throughout your day— when and what you eat and drink, when and how you take breaks and recharge.

Study your patterns. Which ones enable you to be effective or ineffective? More energized or less energized? Experiment with your patterns to determine which ones help you perform at your best. And your worst. Because it's just as important to eliminate negative patterns as it is to develop positive ones.

You might think that maintaining patterns requires discipline. Let's test that. Do you shower or bathe regularly? Does that take discipline or is it a habit? Do you wash your body parts in the same order? Does that take discipline or is it a habit? Once something becomes a habit, there's no decision to make. *It doesn't require discipline.* What takes discipline is to repeat a pattern regularly and often enough so that it becomes a habit.

Not every successful leader has the same patterns, but all successful leaders have patterns. Identifying the patterns that enable you to perform at your best gives you confidence. Consistently applying those patterns makes them habits and demonstrates commitment.

> *Study your patterns. Which ones enable you to be effective or ineffective?*

TAKEAWAYS

- The #1 enemy of commitment is complacency. To defeat it:

  - Continually have an inspiring next goal

  - Create a Personal Case for Change

  - Develop powerful, positive patterns

THE ENEMY THAT GROWS STRONGER BY THE DAY

The difference between successful people and really successful people is that really successful people say no to almost everything.

—Warren Buffett

THEY'RE COMING AT YOU from all directions. They're growing, they're getting stronger, and if you don't avoid them or fend them off, you will fail.

Distractions. It's like you're at the Grand Bazaar with a thousand vendors yelling at you, pulling at you, enticing you with their wares. And it's never-ending.

DON'T CONFUSE DISTRACTIONS WITH DISTRACTIBILITY

Distractions don't torpedo strategy execution; *distractibility* does. Much like the distinction engineers make between stress and strain—stress is the force applied to an object; strain is the response of the object to the applied stress—distractions are what lure your attention; distractibility is how you respond.

It's a choice. Some distractions are obviously a poor use of your time, like mindlessly and excessively wandering through social media. The trickier distractions are the ones you could do, but should you? Like handling a customer issue that could be delegated. Of course, some distractions are truly urgent, requiring you to act *now*, like receiving word that your warehouse is flooding.

Are you *passively distractible*—your attention is easily diverted, or *actively distractible*—you choose to divert your attention when warranted?

MANAGE YOURSELF

Fortunately, there are practices that can help you self-manage and resist distractions.

Prioritize Your Priorities

Use psychology to your advantage. If you simply spend time *working* on a strategic initiative but don't block time to *complete* specific tasks or milestones, then you'll be susceptible to distractions. Because there's no goal and, as a result, no chance to fail and no disincentive to being distracted.

Committing blocks of time to complete specific tasks or milestones creates *positive pressure* and makes you less susceptible to distractions. There's both an incentive—completing the intended task or milestone, and a disincentive—the potential to fail.

If something is truly a priority, then prioritize it. Block time and commit to what you intend to accomplish. You won't be perfect at estimating the time you'll need, and you may not complete everything, but you will build the discipline of prioritizing your priorities and become better at estimating the time you need.

Make and Take Breaks

Making and taking breaks makes you less vulnerable to distractions. If you're skeptical, believing that you don't need to take breaks, then consider this: Research shows that high performers routinely take breaks. A 5-minute walking break every hour helps to boost energy and sharpen focus. And evidence suggests that a 15-minute break, roughly every hour, is best of all.[1]

It's not a matter of *needing* to take breaks; it's a matter of optimizing your performance. If you don't allow time for breaks, then your concentration will wane, and distractions will take hold. Fatigue and boredom affect all of us, and we may not even be aware of it.

Breaks should be guilt-free time to do whatever you want, as frivolous and unproductive as that might be. Play a game. Surf the web. Power nap. Go outside, walk, and stretch.

Schedule fixed breaks. Set alarms to keep yourself from being endlessly immersed in your work. Don't worry, it will still be there when you get back.

Commit to Being 100 Percent Present

Beware. When you get distracted, it negatively affects your team. When you're in a meeting scrolling through texts and bouncing in and out to take calls, what messages are you sending to your team? That the meeting isn't important. That that they aren't important. That you don't really care. Are those the messages you want to send?

The solution is to be *100 percent present.* What messages would you be sending in a meeting if you *listened intensively*, leaning forward, looking directly at the person speaking? If you *asked probing questions* to gain clarity and to understand the thinking behind the speaker's conclusions? If you *thanked people* for their active participation? The first message you would send is that you're engaged. Next, that your behavior is the norm *and* the expectation. Finally, that people need to bring their A game to meetings.

When your team members see you getting distracted, it undermines *their* commitment. If something is important enough for you to be a part of, then don't just go through the motions. Be a role model. Be 100 percent present.

MANAGE THE EXTERNAL DISTRACTIONS

Even if you're doing a good job of self-managing, there are still external forces working to distract you, like ad hoc meetings, communication alerts, and emerging issues.

Corral Your Communications

Be honest with yourself: Constantly monitoring and responding to communications isn't a necessity. It's an obsession. Reacting to every buzz, beep, and flash doesn't make you productive. It makes you Pavlov's dog.

Corral your communications. With rare exception, you don't need to be continuously connected. Block fixed times throughout the day to check your emails, texts, voice mails, digital feeds, etc. Which means you *don't* check them at other times. Corralling your communications will make you feel you're in control of your day and activities.

Be Selectively Inaccessible

Sure, you want to be a leader who's accessible, who people feel comfortable coming to at any time. That's well-intended. The reality is that you can't be a strategic leader *and* be on a leash 24/7. You need dedicated time to think and act. Sometimes, you need to be *inaccessible*.

Are people constantly coming at you? Then block 10 percent of your working time (a half day per week or one day every two weeks) outside of the office so you can devote yourself to strategic activity. Let your team know what you're doing and not to contact you unless it's truly urgent.

What happens when you're at the office? Let's assume you've got a traditional office space with a door. While it's good to have an open-door policy—it shows that you're approachable and that people can drop by and talk about what's on their mind—there are times when you don't want to be interrupted. You need to be free from distractions. Institute an *open-door/closed-door policy*. When your door is open—which should be most of the time— you're accessible. When it's not, you're not. Doing this allows you to take control of your time when you need to, and it lets your team know when you're dealing with something important and shouldn't be interrupted.

What if you're in an open office plan? If the space includes quiet rooms, work pods, or private enclaves, then make use of them. If not, consider using headphones or create some other signal to indicate you're in temporary do-not-disturb mode. In any case, take actions like these sparingly. In your effort to avoid distractions, you don't want to convey to your team that, in general, you're inaccessible.

What do you do when someone approaches you with a non-urgent issue, but it's going to take more time than you have available? Do you attempt to rush through it? Try this instead:

"Matt, this sounds like an important issue. I want to make sure I can give you my full attention and best thinking. Right now isn't that time. Let's pull up our calendars and see if we can block time later today or tomorrow at the latest. Would that work?"

Yes, you want to be a leader who's accessible, but that's only part of the picture. You also want to be an effective strategic leader. To be both, be selectively inaccessible.

Practice 4D Prioritization

How do you decide what to do when requests, tasks, issues, and projects are coming at you from all directions? Do you make good decisions or impulsive decisions? The 4D Prioritization Process, gives you a quick way to make better decisions (see next page). By asking the three questions shown in the figure, you can determine the best course of action in response to any demand.

4D Prioritization Process

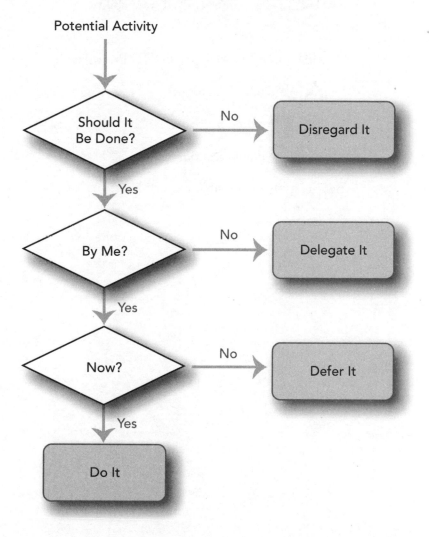

- The #2 enemy of commitment is distractability.
  To defeat it:

  - Prioritize your priorities; practice 4D Prioritization

  - Schedule and take fixed breaks

  - Be 100 percent present

  - Corral your communications

  - Be selectively inaccessible

19

THE ENEMY THAT POSES AS A FRIEND

Mountains have a way of dealing with overconfidence.

—Hermann Buhl

The third enemy you must confront is the most insidious. It makes you feel good, and good about yourself. It poses as a friend. Left unchecked, it will lure you along the path to failure. Ego.

Let's be clear. To be an effective leader you *need* a strong and secure ego. You have to be able to confront tough situations, make painful decisions, overcome massive challenges, and take risks that, even if well calculated, could lead to severe outcomes. And you must have and project confidence through all of it.

Yet it's possible to have a strong ego and *not* be an egomaniac. The question is, are you in control of your ego, or is your ego in control of you?

HOW RUNAWAY EGO POISONS CULTURE AND UNDERMINES EXECUTION

What are the telltale signs that your ego is out of control?

1. You immediately blame others when things go wrong. After all, if they thought it was you who screwed up, they'd lose respect and confidence in you.

    Deflecting responsibility is weakness, not strength. The message you send is that it's everyone for himself and that only losers make mistakes. Congratulations. If your goal is to create a culture in which people fear failure, won't take risks, and cover up mistakes, you've succeeded.

2. You hoard credit for successes. And why not? Someone had to point people in the right direction and light a fire under them. That someone was you.

    Hoarding glory elicits contempt, not admiration. Denying team members the opportunity to be recognized and feel good about their accomplishments all but guarantees they won't give you the same effort next time. Of course, they lose respect for you, because you're self-serving.

3. You don't follow established processes and standards. It's understandable. The only reason they exist is to keep everyone else in line. Besides, it's not against the law when you are the law.

    Double standards demotivate. They create a culture of "us versus them." People bristle when two-faced leaders hold themselves to a different standard just because they can.

4. You conspicuously enjoy the perks of your position, as you should. You've paid your dues. You've put in your time. Now it's their turn to sacrifice.

   Projecting elite status separates you from your team. When people can't identify with their leaders, they don't identify with their leaders' goals. As a result, they're less motivated and less committed.

5. You threaten, berate, extort, or otherwise take inappropriate action to get what you want. Hey, that's life. Sometimes you have to kick a little butt or bend the rules to get results.

   Now they don't just disrespect you; they despise you. And you can be sure they will undermine you every chance they get.

Have you been on the receiving end of any of these? Leaders with runaway egos poison culture and undermine execution. Yes, it's good to have a strong and secure ego. Just make sure your's is under control.

> *Are you in control of your ego,*
> *or is your ego in control of you?*

HOW RUNAWAY EGO IS SELF-LIMITING

When you think you know everything, you're unable to learn anything. In a dynamic environment, if you can't learn, then you can't adapt. And if you can't adapt, then ultimately you'll fail.

When you get smug, thinking you're the best, you have no reason to improve. In a world where the bar is constantly being raised, if you're not improving then you're falling behind. And if you're falling behind then, again, you're on the road to failure.

> When you think you know everything,
> you're unable to learn anything.

Research suggests that companies often fail because leaders become arrogant as a result of their successes.[1] They stop learning, adapting, and improving. Committed leaders want to know what they don't know but *should* know. They willingly own up to what they don't know, which role-models for their team that it's OK not to know everything. As long as you keep learning, adapting, and improving.

THE PARADOX OF VULNERABILITY

Being vulnerable does *not* mean you're incompetent or weak. Paradoxically, being vulnerable can *elevate* how you're perceived as a leader.

For example, taking responsibility for your mistakes enhances your credibility because it sends the message that you're honest and have the courage to admit that you're human. Impress upon your team that making a mistake should trigger two questions: "What did I learn?" and "What would I do differently next time?" By role-modeling that, you start to create a culture of learning and personal responsibility.

Recognizing team members' accomplishments also strengthens your credibility. It sends a message that you value them and that you're secure enough to surround yourself with strong talent. Appreciating their strengths has a similar effect. It sends a message that you don't have to be the best, the smartest, the "whateverest." Like all of us, you have weaknesses. Acknowledge them, and encourage the people on your team to acknowledge their weaknesses.

A TIME FOR VULNERABILITY

Scott, our young CEO-client, was distraught. He had taken over the family business from his father a few years back, and now, for various reasons, the business was in serious trouble. He had little choice but to conduct layoffs. It would be a first for the company, and he struggled knowing the effect it would have on people's lives.

We planned an all-employee meeting at which he would announce what needed to be done and why. He was concerned about getting emotional at the meeting. As we coached him through the preparation, we encouraged him to be real, to acknowledge the gravity of the situation, to take full responsibility, to express confidence that this was the right decision for the company to survive, and to recognize and empathize with what it would mean for the affected employees.

The day of reckoning came. As he spoke about the layoffs and how he empathized with the effect it would have on individual lives, his voice started to falter. Tears welled in his eyes. He said he took it as a personal failure that he had not been able to avoid the situation they were now in, and that he and the company would take specific steps to support the affected employees and ease their transition.

Then something unexpected happened. Employees started to approach the front of the room. Some of the employees who were about to be laid off *consoled him*, thanking him for his openness and his sensitivity. Other employees hugged those employees. Caring and respect permeated the room.

Everyone knew that Scott was being candid and vulnerable. It spoke to his leadership and his character. It was a moment that no one would forget.

TAKEAWAYS

- The #3 enemy of commitment is ego. To control it:
  - Understand that vulnerability can enhance your credibility
  - Acknowledge others' strengths and accomplishments
  - Share credit, don't hoard it
  - Admit mistakes, don't deny them
  - Be more concerned with learning than knowing
- Recognize that it's not *about* you; it's *through* you.

20

THERE'S COMMITMENT; THEN THERE'S *COMMITMENT*

You either commit to mediocrity or commit to greatness.

—Les Brown

AIR TECHNOLOGIES IS NORTH AMERICA'S largest independent distributor and servicer of air compressors. Based in Columbus, Ohio, it is one of those highly successful mid-market companies that, unless you know the industry, you've likely never heard of.

Embracing the principles and practices of ruthless consistency changed the trajectory of this 57-year-old company. As its president, Kurt Lang, noted, "If we didn't adopt ruthless consistency, we wouldn't have achieved the great things we've achieved for well over 10 years."

What Air Technologies achieved over the past 10 years was a 14 percent compound annual growth rate, customer retention that, as Lang described, "aggressively exceeded our aggressive expectations," and a team of people who are "focused, positive, mentally tough, able to execute, and who get fulfillment from their work."

How was Air Technologies able to accomplish all that? Developing the right focus was the foundation—a compelling Case for Change and concise strategic positioning. Lang believed that if Air Technologies committed to ruthless consistency, it could dominate every market in which it chose to compete (the gain). If it didn't, it would be little more than another mediocre company, something he simply couldn't allow himself to accept (the pain). Winning meant dominating every market in which the company chose to compete *because of its customers' choices*. He was clear that the company had to be uncompromisingly customer-focused, and that dominance could only be validated through customer acquisition and customer retention. This was reflected in Air Technologies' Brand Commitment to "LISTEN to what's important to you, COMMIT to solutions that fit your goals, and DELIVER on our promises." To fulfill all of this required a culture committed to the right behaviors, behaviors rooted in values:

Integrity—We will do what we say we will do. Our words and actions will be honest, ethical, and respectful.

Achievement—We will strive for and be judged in our work by our individual and collective accomplishments.

Investment—We believe in our future and will continuously invest in ourselves and our company.

Balance—We will enjoy life by working passionately, playing hard, and loving and appreciating family and friends.

Yet what about purpose? Is there a greater purpose underlying what Air Technologies does? It's a topic Lang feels strongly about: "It isn't just about work. It's about how we're going to provide a better life for our people. We talk about how we're doing this for our team members and their families; they appreciate this and it makes a difference in their lives."

Each fall, Lang works with his team to develop objectives, strategies (SCIs), and plans of attack (Execution Plans) in support of the company's strategic positioning. Past strategies have focused on areas such as employee engagement, customer loyalty, market share, service metrics, pricing strategy, operational efficiency, and gross margin. Progress and accomplishments are tracked in monthly update meetings.

Lang focuses intensively on creating an environment in which everything supports the company's strategic focus. High-level goals are cascaded down the org chart and translated into specific, individual expectations. Air Technologies invests heavily in people, not just in job-related training but in development that helps team members grow and reach their true potential. He brings in top speakers from across North America to discuss the latest concepts, methods, and practices, as well as what he calls "universal training," such as stress management and meditation, to help people manage their lives better. "I want to grow people," he said. "Leaders have a social responsibility to develop better human beings."

Consistent with the Cultural Commitment of "achievement," managers hold monthly coaching meetings with team members to maintain a focus on performance and results. With transparency being the norm, sales, service, and operational ratings for team members are regularly displayed and discussed in group forums. Achievement awards are presented in front of peers to reinforce the importance of accomplishment. As for accountability, Lang explained, "Our people need to feel valued, and if we don't expect more from them, support them, and hold them accountable, they're not going to feel valued."

What if someone doesn't fit the culture? "If a person isn't committed to the customer, doesn't achieve, or doesn't act with integrity—then they're not a fit for our team. And if for some reason we as leaders miss what's happening, the team will make sure we know, and insist the person is removed from the team."

The right focus and right environment are critical, but you still have to build the right team. How has Air Technologies done that? "When we recruit people, we place far more emphasis now on who we are, what our culture demands, and what we're continually working to achieve. We want people who are aligned with our vision of ruthless consistency and who can *prove to us* that they fit.

"Because execution is so important, we ask people about the achievement they're most proud of and what their execution plan was to accomplish it. We want spirit and ambition, but also the courage and discipline to execute and follow through. The profile of the people we've hired over the past 12 years has significantly changed."

Right focus, right environment, right team, and years of success. How does Lang maintain the right commitment? What keeps him from getting complacent? "I have to be the role model," he said. "If I get complacent, then the team gets complacent. There's only one prescription for success and that's consistency. If I'm not consistent—leading by example and working hard—then our people won't be as committed."

What about distractions? "Distractions are a part of life, but you can *choose* whether to be distracted or not. If I get distracted and start letting things slip, my team has the freedom to call me on it. Accountability has to go both ways."

Given everything Air Technologies has achieved, how does Lang keep his ego in check? "It's knowing that there's always room for growth and improvement." He added, "In our culture, any employee can voice their opinion if a leader is getting too full of himself. They can respectfully confront that person without fear of retribution."

Finally, I asked him about the unique challenges of managing in a downturn. It's one thing to be ruthlessly consistent in normal times, but what happens when normal no longer applies? "Without ruthless consistency," he answered, "we would not have been profitable while avoiding layoffs through the downturn of 2008. And there's no way we would have been well positioned to navigate through the coronavirus crisis."

It's easy to be inconsistent. It's a lot harder to be ruthlessly consistent. Leadership expert Jim Collins wrote, "The signature of mediocrity is chronic inconsistency." Yes, and the signature of excellence is ruthless consistency.

What drives all of it is the right commitment. Ask yourself this one question: "Do I have the will to win, or the will *to do what it takes* to win?"

TAKEAWAY

- Commitment. It's a choice.

REFLECTIONS
In the End, It's You Versus You

To be a champion, compete. To be a great champion,
compete with the best. But to be the greatest champion,
compete with yourself.

—Matshona Dhliwayo

IF YOU WANT TO PLAY the odds, bet on failure. If you want to beat the odds, be ruthlessly consistent. Develop and sustain the right focus. Create and keep creating the right environment. Build and keep building the right team.

You can't dabble and expect to win. What matters more than anything you do is *everything* you do. Once you're clear on *why* your organization must change, *what* you intend to achieve, and *how* you intend to achieve it, make certain that every decision and every action is painstakingly aligned with your intentions.

What you do is not as important as what *your people* experience. It's not about you; it's through you. Align their hearts and minds with winning. Equip them, and enable them to succeed. Coach them; don't just manage them. Design your organization to support them, and always value them as individuals, as human beings.

What drives all of this is the consistency of your commitment. Either elevate your commitment to what is required to win, or redefine winning to match your commitment. One or the other.

There will be many challenges—obstacles, setbacks, and frustrations—but they won't determine your success. Because in the end, it's not you versus those challenges. It's you versus you.

ACKNOWLEDGMENTS

I FIRMLY BELIEVE that it takes a team. Any individual accomplishment reflects the influence of many people who, in ways great or small, obvious or subtle, deliberate or unintended, helped shape the outcome.

Jan Bundy, my Business Manager at Making Strategy Happen, has provided tremendous support over the years. Her diligence, integrity, and professionalism have given me the peace of mind to focus on what I should be focused on: consulting, speaking, and writing. I'm very fortunate to have her both as a team member and a trusted friend.

Katt Stearns, my Director of Digital Marketing, has skillfully established and grown my presence in the digital world along with being a talented and committed Project Manager. She is truly a pleasure to work with. Jessica Wiser, my Social Media Manager, has joyfully complemented Katt's efforts by coordinating my social media presence and engagement. And my sister, Cyndi Canic, has provided much-valued administrative support with her usual "walking on sunshine" spirit.

One of the best decisions I made was to hire Dianna Booher as my "Book Coach." Dianna's experience and expertise have been invaluable. Thanks to her efforts, my book proposal attracted the attention of Carol Mann, who generously agreed to act as my agent. Thanks to Carol's efforts, the proposal spurred the interest of major publishers, and once I spoke with Casey Ebro, Executive Editor at McGraw Hill, I was convinced I had found the right partner. I owe much to Casey and her team, whose energy and expertise have helped turn my original manuscript into a much stronger finished product. Patty Wallenburg deserves special mention. I should also acknowledge my former teacher and now friend, Barrie Street, whose sharp eye for detail helped tighten the manuscript.

One of my objectives was to give the book a "fighting chance to be commercially successful." To this end, I knew I needed top-tier publicity and marketing support. I'm confident I chose the right partners in Mark Fortier and his team at Fortier Public Relations and Ken Gillett and his team at Target Marketing to augment the solid efforts of the team at McGraw Hill.

There is a long, long list of clients, colleagues, and friends who have inspired, influenced, and challenged my thinking. This book is a testament to all of them. Ultimately, the words on these pages reflect their experiences and insights as much as mine. Arthur Stanley and Hyler Bracey deserve special recognition.

Back when I was studying the psychology of human performance and learning how to think, I benefitted greatly from the insights, guidance, and support of many first-rate professors, including my doctoral supervisor, Ian Franks. I also had the opportunity to apply much of what I learned while coaching football at the University of British Columbia. Working under Head Coach Frank Smith, and winning a national championship, I learned firsthand the importance of building the right team, developing the right focus, and creating the right environment—ruthless consistency.

"Focus, motivation, organization, discipline" is a mantra I repeat frequently. I have been deeply inspired by my grandfather

Ivan Canic's focus, my father's motivation, my mother's organization, and my Uncle Tony's legendary discipline.

In a life of incomprehensible good luck, most improbable of all is that I found the amazing Bernadine, who has been my teammate in life, love, and adventure for over 30 years. And what an adventure it's been. I could not have imagined a better life partner, and I could not have done what I've done without her.

APPENDIX

All the models, forms, and questionnaires in this book can be accessed at:

RuthlessConsistency.com
(Password: MakeItHappen)

List of downloadable content:

Ruthless Consistency model
Strategic Management Process model
Execution Plan template
Resource Matrix template
Measurement Matrix template
Analysis-Action Ladder
Master Calendar template
Engagement-Performance model
Alignment Questionnaire—Leaders
Alignment Questionnaire—Team Members
Converging Evidence model
4D Prioritization Process

You'll find more helpful resources on Michael's website:

MichaelCanic.com

NOTES

Introduction

1. Perhaps the most oft-cited source is: Robert S. Kaplan and David P. Norton, *The Strategy-Focused Organization*, Harvard Business School Press, 2000.
2. Clayton M. Christensen, Richard Alton, Curtis Rising, and Andrew Waldeck, "The Big Idea: The New M&A Playbook," *Harvard Business Review*, March 2011.
3. Richard S. McLean, Jiju Antony, and Jens J. Dahlgaard, "Failure of Continuous Improvement Initiatives in Manufacturing Environments: A Systematic Review of the Evidence," *Total Quality Management & Business Excellence*, August 6, 2015, pp. 219–237 (https://www.tandfonline.com/doi/abs/10.1080/1478 3363.2015.1063414).
4. "Standish Group 2015 Chaos Report—Q&A with Jennifer Lynch" (https://www.infoq.com/articles/standish-chaos -2015/).
   Unsuccessful projects were classified as either "challenged" or "failed." Just over 70 percent fell into this combined category.
5. Michael Krigsman, "Worldwide Cost of IT Failure (Revisited): $3 Trillion," ZDNet, April 10, 2012 (https://www.zdnet.com/ article/worldwide-cost-of-it-failure-revisited-3-trillion/).
6. Ron Ashkenas, "Change Management Needs to Change," *Harvard Business Review*, April 16, 2013 (https://hbr.org/ 2013/04/change-management-needs-to-cha).

Chapter 2

1. Tony Alessandra and Michael O'Connor, *The Platinum Rule: Discover the Four Basic Business Personalities and How They Can Lead You to Success*, Time Warner Publishing, 1996.
2. Several related sources speak to this research:
   Michael Bush and Sarah Lewis-Kulin, "The 100 Best Companies to Work For: Why They Matter," *Fortune*, March 9, 2017 (https://fortune.com/2017/03/09/best-companies-2017-intro/).
   Also: Michael Bush and Sarah Lewis-Kulin, "Here's How to Get on Our Best Companies to Work For List," *Fortune*, March 9, 2017; (https://fortune.com/2017/03/09/best-companies-list-how-to/).
   And: Michael C. Bush, *A Great Place to Work For All*, Berrett-Koehler Publishers, Inc., 2018.
3. Ibid.
4. Ibid.

Chapter 5

1. "Prospect Theory," which addresses psychological asymmetries in how we assess prospective gain and loss, won Kahneman the Nobel Prize in Economics in 2002.
2. Salvatore Calabrese, *Cognac: A Liquid History*, Cassell, 2001.

Chapter 6

1. Jim Collins, *How the Mighty Fall: And Why Some Companies Never Give In*, Jim Collins, 2009.
2. Darrell Rigby and Barbara Bilodeau, "Management Tools & Trends: Five Key Trends Emerged from Bain's Survey of 1,268 Managers," Bain & Company, April 5, 2018 (https://www.bain.com/insights/management-tools-and-trends-2017/).

Chapter 7

1. W. Chan Kim and Renee Mauborgne, *Blue Ocean Strategy* (rev. ed.), Harvard Business Review Press, 2015.
2. Jeanne Hardy, "Strategic Leadership: The Strategy of Saying No," Business 2 Community, October 9, 2019. (Business2community.com/strategy/strategic-leadership-the-strategy-of-saying-no-02247415).

3. James Clear, "Warren Buffett's '2 List' Strategy: How to Maximize Your Focus and Master Your Priorities," (https://jamesclear.com/buffett-focus).

Chapter 9

1. Daniel Pink makes a strong case for how we over-rely on money as a motivator in *Drive: The Surprising Truth About What Motivates Us*, Riverhead Books, 2009.

Chapter 10

1. James D. Kirkpatrick and Wendy Kayser Kirkpatrick, *Kirkpatrick's Four Levels of Training Evaluation*, ATD Press, 2016.

Chapter 11

1. The expert on "deliberate practice" is K. Anders Ericsson. The best source I have come across on expertise and performance is: K. Anders Ericsson, Robert R. Hoffman, Aaron Kozbelt, and A. Mark Williams (eds.), *The Cambridge Handbook of Expertise and Expert Performance* (2nd ed.), Cambridge University Press, 2018.
2. "Performance Review Peril: Adobe Study Shows Office Workers Waste Time and Tears," January 11, 2017 (https://news.adobe.com/news/news-details/2017/Performance-Review-Peril-Adobe-Study-Shows-Office-Workers-Waste-Time-and-Tears/default.aspx).
   The study may be relatively recent, but the spirit of the findings is not. Gary Markle, author of *Catalytic Coaching: The End of the Performance Review* (Praeger, 2000), has been making the case for over 20 years that the downsides of performance reviews far outweigh their upsides.
3. The SMART acronym—specific, measurable, achievable, relevant, and time-bound—is commonly used for goal-setting criteria. I use the variation shown when referring to feedback and guidance.
4. Frederick Herzberg, Bernard Mausner, and Barbara Snyderman, *The Motivation to Work* (2nd ed.), John Wiley, 1959. This work was revisited and summarized in Frederick Herzberg, "One More Time: How Do You Motivate Employees?," *Harvard Business Review*, vol. 46 (1), pp. 53–62, 1968.

5. Marcus Buckingham and Curt Coffman, *First, Break All the Rules: What the World's Greatest Managers Do Differently*, Simon & Schuster, 1999.
6. Daniel H. Pink, *Drive: The Surprising Truth About What Motivates Us*, Riverhead Books, 2009.
7. A bonus plan that reinforces *process*, not just *results*, of course requires financial guardrails. A common guardrail is that a bonus of any sort is paid out only if the company generates a predetermined amount of net income. It also requires management rigor, so that check-the-box plans and trivial actions aren't rewarded. As for percentages, you might start by allocating 10 percent for a well-conceived and documented plan, 15 percent for demonstrated execution, and 75 percent for achieving results.

Chapter 13

1. Mary Hayes, Fran Chumney, Corinne Wright, and Marcus Buckingham, "The Global Study of Engagement," ADP Research Institute, 2019 (https://www.adp.com/-/media/adp/ResourceHub/pdf/ADPRI/ADPRI0100_2018_Engagement_Executive_Summary_RELEASE%20READY.ashx).

Chapter 14

1. There aren't good data that speak to how long a person will spend looking for "careers," or a similar link on a web page, before losing interest. Various online sources have suggested that, in general, you have 5 to 15 seconds to capture a person's attention on a web page; yet the research behind these numbers, if it even exists, is poorly referenced. I've picked 10 seconds, the midpoint in the range, simply to make the point.
2. Richard Branson, "Look after your staff," Virgin, March 27, 2014 (https://www.virgin.com/richard-branson/look-after-your-staff).

Chapter 15

1. Ian MacRae, Adrian Furnham, and Martin Reed, *High Potential: How to Spot, Manage and Develop Talented People at Work, 2nd ed.*, Bloomsbury, 2018.
2. Carol S. Dweck, *Mindset: The New Psychology of Success* (updated ed.), Ballantine Books, 2007.

Chapter 17

1. Jo Ellison, "Karl Lagerfeld: King of Couture," *Financial Times*, July 3, 2015 (https://www.ft.com/content/6c312fe6-1e47 -11e5-aa5a-398b2169cf79).
2. Ibid.
3. According to author Tim Ferris, who interviewed more than 200 world-class performers and experts, 80 percent of those experts meditate.

Chapter 18

1. Daniel H. Pink, *Drive: The Scientific Secrets of Perfect Timing*, Riverhead Books, 2018

Chapter 19

1. Jim Collins, *How the Mighty Fall: And Why Some Companies Never Give In*, Jim Collins, 2009.

INDEX

ABOUT THE AUTHOR

MICHAEL CANIC, PHD, is the president of Making Strategy Happen, a consulting firm that helps committed leaders of mid-market companies turn ambition into strategy, and strategy into reality. Previously, he managed the consulting division at The Atlanta Consulting Group. He also held a leadership role at FedEx, where his district became the most recognized in the Americas for service quality.

A compelling speaker, he has delivered more than 600 presentations to audiences on four continents, many through Vistage Worldwide which, with over 24,000 members in 20+ countries, is the world's largest organization of CEOs and business leaders.

Michael is a former national championship-winning college football coach. He is a member of Marshall Goldsmith's 100 Coaches global initiative.

An adventure traveler, he and wife, Bernadine, have been to more than 40 countries. He has summited numerous peaks in the Andes, journeyed by camel in the Sahara, trekked the mountains of Northern Pakistan, and swum with piranha in the Amazon.

For more information, please visit MichaelCanic.com.